Letting Go
and
Moving On

Letting Go
and Moving On

Easing Retirement for Professional Men and Their Wives

Dwight Hervey Small

Baker Books

A Division of Baker Book House Co.
Grand Rapids, Michigan 49516

Published by Baker Books,
a division of Baker Book House Company
PO Box 6287, Grand Rapids, Michigan 49516-6287

Printed in the United States of America

Library of Congress Cataloging-in-Publication Data

Small, Dwight Hervey.
    Letting go and moving on : easing retirement for professional men and their wives / Dwight Hervey Small.
      p.   cm.
    Includes bibliographical references.
    ISBN 0-8010-8343-5
    1. Retirees—Religious life. 2. Married people—Religious life. 3. Retirement—Psychological aspects. I. Title.
    BV4596.R47S63   1993
    248.8'5—dc20   93-3983

To

T. G. Torvik

Faithful friend
True pastor
There for me

Contents

Acknowledgments

Two special people at Baker deserve
the author's gratitude.

Dan Van't Kerkhoff, editor, general trade books,
caught the author's vision and believed in his message
when the manuscript was still in embryonic form.
He patiently mentored the project
through many intermediate stages,
offering invaluable suggestions at every juncture.

Mary Suggs, assistant managing editor,
undertook the editorial process but did much more.
She sensitively labored to fully understand
the special focus of the book,
corrected its need for substantial reorganization,
and proceeded to craft the wording
with her own magic, putting the stamp of order
and clarity on every page.

Introduction

Two weeks is about the ideal length of time to retire." So said Alex Comfort, the renowned gerontologist.[1] Does he have a point? Ask men now retired from professional or business careers. Many will answer "Yes." And behind each "yes" are reasons as diverse as the men answering.

Comfort's arresting comment points to a severe problem that applies especially to men leaving business or professional careers in which they've had significant public prominence—high visibility individuals. For them, the threat is that of comprehensive personal dislocation, and the likely prospect of inner disorientation as well as outward dislocation.

Life as they've known it has come to an abrupt end; for many it's no less than an upheaval of traumatic proportions. One world has literally been exchanged for another, one way of life left behind for another. The bridge between the two is less than firm beneath their feet, and at best, things are to an extent uncertain.

In the mid-1970s a team from the University of Washington interviewed 5,000 individuals and established the Holmes-Rahe Scales of Social Adjustment, which measures the stressors caused by varying events in a person's life. Events are assigned a certain number of stress units. Retirement garners forty-three units. Add to that the accompanying stress factors, such as relocation, and it's easy to accumulate the 300 units that are said to bring about a major crisis.

Books that will prepare one for retirement are plentiful. In terms of the pragmatic, programmable aspects, these subjects are amply covered in a vast literature available to retirees. Few of these books deal with the psychological aspects of retirement—the inner journey with its special hazards. Add to this the spiritual needs and challenges to Christian retirees, and we encounter another dimension altogether.

So what is it about retirement that renders men suddenly vulnerable in strange new ways, prone to deep inner disturbance and unsettledness? How are they to handle radical change and inevitable losses? Practical answers make up the easier part; coping with inner changes is the tough part.

For each individual, it's not what happens with external circumstances that's of greatest concern, but what happens internally—what takes place in the mind and emotions, the subtle and not-so-subtle psychological dynamics at play. Also, what happens to alter close relationships.

My intent, then, is not primarily to propose "successful strategies for smooth sailing." Nor is my aim to outline the how-to's of retirement adjustment. Rather, my major objective is to examine and understand the inner journey with its particular spiritual and psychological needs, and then to show how God provides for these needs through the adequacy of life in Christ.

I write from my own experience, having retired from a career in the ministry and as a college professor, author, and national seminar speaker and having experienced a delayed post-retirement crisis. I believe there is universal significance in aspects of my experience as it applies to leaving a public career.

For a host of men leaving professional or business careers there are no simple strategies for achieving a settled, successful new life. It is most important that these men be aware of the nature of the psychological booby traps awaiting them, including pitfalls of their own making. So the heart of this book is, "How can I safely cross this bridge to retirement (and in the process grow into mature Christian personhood), make the most of who I am in the Lord, and fulfill my remaining potential for a life of service as God enables me?" A rather large order!

What matters most is how we cope with the unexpected and unplanned for, especially the abrupt and irreversible nature of the retirement transition. This transition has both similarities and dissimilarities with every other major adult transition.

For many men, to leave what has been their vocation throughout adult years and exchange this for something for which there has been neither training nor adequate preparation can be, and often is, traumatic. As has been remarked, "In our competence centered, competitive oriented, vocational orientation, we've become 'human doings' rather than 'human beings.'" When the "doing" comes to a halt with retirement, we lose our self-identification. Men are not psychologically prepared for this.

Furthermore, to suppose that retirement's an automatic, simple cakewalk into a brightly beckoning world of unmitigated bliss, free forever of all former problems, is the cruelest deceit of all.

In the larger sense, while wishing to know all that retirement embraces pragmatically, of greater import are the things that matter most in personal terms. For example, what meaning does retirement have for Christian men that it does not have for non-Christian men? In other words, for the final staging of earthly existence, what are the spiritual parameters within which a Christian retiree ought to live out his years successfully and joyfully?

The message of the book, while directed to men, is also aimed at spouses who have to live with their retired husbands, all the while making their own difficult adjustments to their husband's retirement, aware of the ramifications for their own lives. Of course, now more than ever, women retiring from similar positions should find the themes of the book highly relevant to them as well, understanding, of course, that the book is written from the focus of the author's male perspective.

All the uncertainty and apprehension a man feels,

his wife feels with him. Everything affecting him, affects her also. Her privacy and autonomy cannot remain the same after her husband has shifted his daily routines to the home, which through all their married years has been under her management. He's invaded her turf and claims equal time there. This calls for the restructuring of her daily patterns to adapt to the new conditions imposed by his retirement. Additionally, adjusting to the added demands of full-time closeness is also something they both face together. So to wives, those important partners-in-retirement, this book also speaks.

Take the matter of dependency/interdependency. What are the new parameters for him, for her? As a fully equal partner, she must structure her independence in conjunction with his. In turn, he must accommodate to this, knowing himself to be no more than an equal partner. His vocational management skills are not meant to transfer over to her domain thus to fill the vacuum he's experiencing. He doesn't resume his place—executive, foreman, lawyer, health provider, or man in the pulpit—in a new location!

Marital strains previously repressed are nearer the surface now. It might take little for these to erupt. Tensions never before experienced are now very real. If, in addition, she must be part of moving to a new location, a new home—perhaps having to give up a vocational position of her own before she's ready to do so—this too, will add to the strain. Now she is suffering directly some of the same detachments as he.

All this in combination puts two people on the edge of disorientation and possible conflict.

Additionally, if because of her husband's isolation from past connections there is now a new dependence on her for finding fulfillment, the wife acquires the further burden of having to become more to him emotionally and socially than ever before. Professionals and businessmen leave both the emotional and the social support indigenous to their careers. In these respects, the spousal relationship may prove increasingly vulnerable to stress. The comfortably worked out balance of mutual autonomy, self-fulfillment, marital accommodation is easily upset by the unexpected new tensions created.

For these and other reasons, if a wife is to assist her husband to make a successful passage into retirement, she needs to understand transition dynamics. The book is designed to be sensitive to, and speak to, her needs as well as his.

Several books have had a decided influence on the writing of this one. I recommend Jules Z. Willing's *The Reality of Retirement*.[2] To Willing especially (and to other writers whose works will be cited), the author is in grateful debt.

The experience of retirement is disruptive, often causing an individual to become disconnected and lose self-definition, but happily, for the Christian, the last word is not negation, but a resounding affirmation of God's power to reintroduce hope and purpose to any man who submits his life to him for this final stretch of the road.

1

Blind-sided
by Status Change

For many American men, that unique, unrepeatable day of retirement, no matter how long they've anticipated it, comes as an event unlike any other they've ever before experienced, softened only by the ritual leave-taking that attends it and the euphoria that obscures the uncertainties ahead.

Typically, men for whom this transition is most difficult are found in middle or upper echelon positions in the professions or in corporate life. Not a few have reached the higher rungs on the ladder of achievement and reward. Some are men whose names emblazon corporate letterhead.

As in my case, some retirees were previously ministers, some having served large congregations. Others were well-positioned as Christian leaders or served on faculties of Christian institutions of higher learning. What these men share in common is their status and public visibility.

For all these men, the actual day of retiring has intriguing similarities. The eventful day arrives with a man, perhaps never before nostalgic about his own career, fighting a lump in the throat and moist eyes. He empties the drawers of his desk, cleans out the files, discards a mountain of stuff he never thought he'd ever do without. There are the degree certificates and the achievement plaques on the wall, the thirtieth-year-anniversary gift desk set. While little of what he keeps has intrinsic value, it's too much to expect that he'll discard it all just now. He packs years of memorabilia in boxes labeled "to go." Just packing it up is enough to trigger a case of separation anxiety.

For the last time, he locks the door, with contrived casualness repeats some good-byes for the second or third time, and just walks away from it all. Taking the first step into untested waters, he's joining the ranks of retirees.

Great day!

But wait! Why the sudden surge of ambivalent feelings?

Almost immediately, in ways he couldn't have imagined just weeks before, status begins to erode. His self-definition is already beginning to suffer shock symptoms.

Watch out! Somebody's about to be blind-sided, hit by enormous status change!

Looked at from this threshhold, is it possible to characterize the essence of the new life in a sentence?

Is it freedom at last—the heralded "life of Riley"—the life of leisure? Is it the chance to live out one's personal dreams—"the best of times" (no longer "yet to be")? Or the opportunity "to do all the things I never had time for"?

How do we characterize retirement, save as each individual does so by his own measuring rod? What has it to do with status? With familiar roles? Daily routines?

Other questions arise. Is there productive life after a career? How do professional or business types restructure their world beyond careers? Around what center will life be organized from now on?

What about Christian men? Are their adjustments different? Do they have prospects not available to non-Christian men? What special conditions come with their special worldview? Is retirement seen as affording opportunity to spend time growing spiritually, perhaps finding greater freedom for service to God? How are these things sorted out and determined?

Passage through Successive Seasons

In the mid-seventies, Gail Sheehy popularized the term "passages" in a book based on a ten-year study by a team led by Daniel Levinson. By "passages" Sheehy meant the movement from one life stage to another. Levinson also wrote a book, which he called *The Seasons of a Man's Life*. We still speak today of "seasons" of life and of the "passages" between. One of those seasons in a man's life is retirement and the passage into this season takes considerable energy. Today a host of women are also making the passage from high-visibility positions to retirement. *Transitions: Making Sense of Life's Changes* is an excellent study by William Bridges in which he gives substance to the lines from T. S. Eliot in *Little Gidding*: "What we call the beginning is often the end. And to make an end is to make a beginning. The end is where we start from."

Bridges elaborates on the idea that a person does not begin a new phase of life without first closing off many present commitments and leaving many primary attachments to people and places.[1] This transition follows a four-step progression, summarized here:

1. *Detachment*. A retiree leaves the people who've been his associates in the working world. This group must be replaced with new, significant associations if the retiree is not to suffer negative responses to the change. Before he can fill the void with a new group, however, he must have a sense of closure of the former relationships. Detachment, separating from them, is the first necessary step.

2. *Repositioning*. People in social systems are organized in hierarchies, each person having his or her position and rank (the pecking order). His or her place in the hierarchy tells a person—and everyone else—who he is and where he belongs. Identity and position provide our primary and secondary attachments. Our attachments are primarily people, but all that makes up the organizational structure forms a part. When a person retires, he or she undergoes change in both position and rank. Depending on where he is

repositioned in the hierarchy, he may have to acquire new skills for the new status that he takes on. This repositioning cannot take place completely until there has been an acceptable closure with past status.

3. *Disorientation.* The sense here is the opposite of orientation. We orient ourselves around our careers and so, by them, we measure the progress of our lives. When we retire we must disorient ourselves from those careers. They no longer can be used to measure our lives. There comes an end beyond which no further progress is to be made and measured. The symbols that measured achievement (all facets of self-definition) now face closure. The symbols of orientation must undergo the process of disorientation before we can genuinely move ahead to new status, new self-definition. In other words, disorientation comes before orientation in this transition—the end before the beginning.

4. *Disconfirmation.* In the transition period marked by closure, we need also to disconfirm the past—a necessary step we take mentally. Here we face our rationalizations about where we are and deal with them honestly. Disconfirmation comes to terms with the realities, preparing us to exchange some realities for others. Confirmation of new realities follows disconfirmation of past ones.

Bridges affirms that closure and disconfirmation necessarily come before a new beginning. This may seem like putting the cart before the horse; it's not. In progressing through major life-transitions, endings come first—endings before beginnings.

For some individuals, these transitions (or passages) are seemingly unexceptional. For others—as in my case—they seem altogether exceptional, often painfully and deceptively so! They're disruptive, even to the point of bringing on a state of depression and dysfunction. Of course, no two men have identical histories, nor do their transitions incorporate identical elements, hence different degrees of difficulty are to be expected.

The Bridge between Stages

A major life-transition is the bridge between two distinct stages of life. This involves moving out of one stage of relative stability and certainty; passing through a brief period of change, loss, and uncertainty; then once again establishing oneself in a new stage marked by relative stability and certainty. It isn't possible to be in two stages at the same time, and bridging the two means briefly occupying an unfamiliar, untested neutral zone in between. It is while occupying that in-between zone that life is fraught with disturbing uncertainty.

Since individuals and circumstances differ widely, many factors affect the retirement transition, and the degree of difficulty each man faces during his passage between the two worlds cannot be accurately predicted. What we do know is that every human experience, like every human being, is unique. Also, the older a person is, the more defined and concretized is his individuality, a condition usually reaching its high point at retirement age, so each retiree writes his own unique narrative, with his unique problems and solutions. Each individual enters retirement on his own terms, making each case an isolated one to be viewed independently of all others. When mention is made in this book of typical backgrounds, typical needs, typical potential, typical hazards, typical possibilities, and typical solutions, the reader must attempt to translate those general terms into the particulars of his own life situation.

In the bridging process, we reposition ourselves, to use Bridges' term. We position ourselves as permanent exiles, away from the world in which we formerly spent most of our waking hours. We move into the neutral zone, no longer living intermittently in two different worlds—the career world of life with work associates set against the private world of family and friends, no longer experiencing the rhythm of dual existence. As Jules Willing puts it, we "move completely into the smaller quarters of our private life."

First Casualty: Status

When an American business or professional man steps into retirement as the final transition of earthly life, he finds himself in an entirely different universe with a lifestyle all its own. He may quickly discover this to be far more difficult and unsure in some respects than previous transitions. There are bound to be features that upset his psychological equilibrium and create fear. Familiar supports are wiped away.

Perhaps here we should note that some writers refer

to death as the last great transition, and in a sense this is correct. When we talk here about "adult transitions," however, what concerns us are only those stages that can be examined to determine how well a person adapts to leaving old attachments and entering new ones, how they've gone on through adapting to new conditions. In our study, we stop short of the transition into eternity because the eternal state is not one that can be examined (although gloriously anticipated!).

What is perhaps the hardest for each man to swallow is the realization that, no matter what his position in the hierarchy may have been, he is no longer "the indispensable man." He no longer retains his long-term, rock-solid status. Everything that once depended on his presence and his abilities no longer depends on him at all. He discovers on his first visit back: "We're getting along just fine, thank you!" As someone remarked, "They give you the watch; then they give you the works!" So the first casualty of retirement is status.

Harder still to swallow, as Willing points out, is the realization that the contributions a man has made to the professional or business world—once gratefully credited to him—are no longer important to anyone but himself, however significant those contributions might have been. His input to the organization has been rapidly surpassed by new issues being tackled, new advances being made, new methods being learned, new solutions in the works. Things are now in the hands of new people—people he doesn't know.

His name carries no weight. Corporate life is moving on without him, and as time passes, the value of what he's worked so hard to accomplish seems to be diminishing in light of the swift changes now occurring. To have one's work devalued because of its fading significance is to feel one's self devalued. Nothing yet designed can soften that blow.

Just when our self-esteem needs to be shored up by recognition of what we've contributed in our day, our accomplishments are losing significance. After all, who gets excited about past achievements? The challenge lies ahead. It is, says Willing, "as though one's contribution has been cancelled from history. His professional life has already suffered death."[2]

James Thorson of the University of Nebraska comments that retirement adjustment "may be better if one is a 'never was' rather than a 'has been.'"

Changing Role of Work

Retirement is self-occupation. It is like work in that it involves a person's talents and it takes preparation and dedication if rewards are to be received. Retirement is a person's occupation as well as his lifestyle and in retirement he must learn to live with leisure rather than with scheduled, structured work.

Part of adapting to the new status of retirement is the importance of this changing role of work. Business and professional men hold positions of prominence and power, exercising leadership in their field. They are voices of authority, individuals to whom other people look. Work itself is deeply immersed in a social network tailored to one's particular occupational milieu. But in retirement, each faces a radical reduction of official involvements and relationships. This causes work to take on a whole new meaning. It also requires different planning.

If in retirement men no longer hold positions of prominence, no longer wield the same authority, they will not be looked to in the same manner as before. As a result, more often than not, self-esteem is lessened. Use of talents is greatly reduced if not eliminated altogether. Everything about the transition is life-negating and detrimental to a sense of self-worth. Not easy to handle, now that the support structures of one's working world have all but disappeared. If work was indeed the very essence of status, where will status reside from now on?

Men are stunned by any abrupt and total status change. Once a man is retired, he begins to think of the years he spent getting an education, advancing a career, honing abilities to manage, motivate, and manipulate. He carved out a whole way of life around the use of his skills, which brought him opportunities for advancement, responsibilities, and rewards.

Then suddenly it's all over and his valued skills go unused. He finds himself asking, "To what purpose is all this, if my most serious decisions from now on are going to be between playing a round of golf, puttering in the garden, watching TV, catching up with *Sports Illustrated*, or reading the latest Tom Clancy novel? Is this the peak I was meant to reach? C'mon, it's the big letdown!"

Setting Retirement Goals

The person who retires must struggle to accept the irreversible change and irretrievable loss indigenous to this stage of his life. He must resist trying to turn back, trying to relive a past forever gone.

There's no escaping the radical changes accompanying retirement. One executive put it this way: "All I've got left is my future!" Another remarked, "I feel like I'm a missing person waiting to be found." A third man wistfully quipped, "Ah, yes, I have a wonderful future behind me!" And from still another comes the comment, "Retirement's not been a picnic!"

Well, if for some business and professional types retirement has not been a picnic, then we need to know which strategies to adopt to successfully move forward through the transition.

One perspective that ensures a successful passage is the ability to see the period just ahead as part of the continuum of your life and so a part of what's being left behind. Preparation should be made in anticipation of the transition into retirement. Potential purposes and patterns should be investigated and plans made that when completed will give a sense of fulfillment.

Each retiree makes a transition from something to something else. It's the "to something else" that's often unclear and hence ill-prepared for. Sometimes there is a considered option chosen for retirement years that later turns out to be unsuitable, requiring still another choice to take its place. Thus retirement is often fraught with false starts.

If we're not to be blind-sided by this major status

change, we need to know fairly accurately what it is toward which we're moving. We need to have some goal in mind if we're to make a good choice and move on with adequate preparation. Before goal-setting, we should interview individuals who've successfully made the passage and evaluate how well they're getting along in their new circumstances. Our assessment should include knowledge of their lives before retirement as well as now. In this fashion we let them show the way, both in positive and negative terms.

So here we are; we envision retirement as the great, final move from all that "was then" to "whatever shall be now." The first hurdle to be surmounted is that of changed status. We must accept the fact that our former status must be relinquished in order to take on whatever new status emerges at the far end of the transition. We must accept that our work and our lifestyle are now one, and we must make informed plans for the future. It can be an exciting adventure of anticipation and realization.

> Lord, give me faith! to live from day to day,
> With tranquil heart to do my simple part,
> And, with hand in Thine, just go Thy way.
>
> Lord, give me faith! to trust, if not to know;
> With quiet mind in all things Thee to find,
> And, childlike, go where Thou wouldst have me go.
>
> Lord, give me faith! to leave it all with Thee.
> The future is Thy gift, I would not lift
> The veil Thy love has hung 'twixt it and me.
>
> John Oxenham[3]

2

How the Self
Is Defined

For those who haven't studied sociology or have only a vague memory of their introduction to a sociology course in college, here is a concise review of a very important sociological aspect touched on in the last chapter—statuses and roles.

Socialization has to do with how the self develops, how we become the people we are. Why do we behave as we do in relation to other people, especially in social groups where we are participants? In what way is our self-definition formed not only by psychological but sociological factors?

We Are Our Statuses

Early on, study of the socialization process introduces us to how individuals are assigned certain statuses and how in turn these statuses are acted out in certain appropriate "roles." Personal development depends on a fundamental congruity between a status and its role-performance. Similarly, any incongruity between the two results in the development of an unstable self and can lead to status disorientation and to role dysfunction.

Commonly, although incorrectly, we hear the word "status" used in reference to prominence or prestige. A well-known figure is said to "have status." This is not, however, the way sociologists use the term. Rather, status has to do with the rank that each person has within a particular social group. Status is a ranking in relation to other group members, with some ranked higher or lower. Since everyone is a part of more than one social group, every individual occupies not one but a number of distinct statuses.

Some Statuses Are "Ascribed"

Statuses fall into two categories. Some are "ascribed," assigned by the social order on the basis of an agreed on classification. Ascribed statuses have nothing to do with personal achievement but are givens. Examples would be gender and ethnicity— statuses not subject to change.

Though we have no control over these statuses, they have a lot to do with what roles we can play in life. In America, the fact that my ascribed status is that of a white male has positive significance for roles I may expect to play (doors I'm able to open). I might also have the ascribed status of "son of a well-to-do family" (I only wish so!). That would open other doors.

Some Statuses Are "Achieved"

Our study really has nothing to do with ascribed statuses but rather with this second category—"achieved statuses." These are earned (they can also be lost or relinquished). The crisis of retirement adjustment has to do with "achieved status loss" and its compensating exchange of new statuses for old ones. This, we shall see, virtually decimates the roles we are used to playing.

Achieved statuses are not static self-definitions. From time to time they undergo change—some are lost, others gained. At any given time, within a person's several social settings (whether formal or informal), his or her statuses are what determine his or her overall self-definition.

For example, a clerk has lower status in his law firm's hierarchy than a lawyer in the same office. The clerk has his own particular status, albeit ranked lower.

His occupational status is not the whole story of the clerk's statuses. He may also be chairman of United Way in his city, thus giving him a higher status in the community, even above that of his office colleague, the lawyer.

A Master-Status

At any given time one particular status is dominant. It is the overriding one, by which we are best known. This is called the master-status. However well-established this status may become, over time and with changing conditions a master-status is likely to change. This commonly occurs to career status and to other statuses as well.

To illustrate, in late teens one's master-status may be "college student," then later perhaps "graduate student." Then it might change to "lawyer," later still to "law partner" in such-and-such a legal firm. A few years later the master-status may be circuit court judge. Here the status takes on wider community prestige. This process is called status ascendancy. An ascending master-status (as with a descending master-status) can at some point be lost, rescinded, or relinquished.

The Effect of Status Movement

While the master-status undergoes change over time, many other statuses either remain the same or independently change too. Professional advancement may alter one's career status, but other statuses, such as that of husband, father, golf partner, church elder, or community leader will remain the same or change independently of career status.

Our concern here is the impact of master-status change. The master-status of one of the best-known figures of our time, Ronald Reagan, changed through the years. At one time his master-status was sportscaster. Later it was Hollywood actor, then governor of California. At one time it was candidate for president of the United States, and eventually president. Following eight years of highest national status, Ronald Reagan's status is now former president of the

United States. His master-status rose through numerous transitions, then abruptly descended when he left the presidency. His master-status can never again ascend to where it was.

Whenever a person moves from a lesser to a greater master-status, the former status is usually left behind with little personal adjustment; there is no reason to desire its return. But to move from a greater to a lesser master-status can pose a critical problem of adjustment. This can be true with occupational demotion, with being benched on the church baseball team, replaced as adult Bible class teacher, or not reelected to the city council. Since being retired is generally considered a lesser status than working as a professional, adjustment may follow a crisis of status on the heels of retirement.

The abrupt change in master-status leaves one unfulfilled, even when other statuses remain significant. Immediately there occurs a sudden disorganization of roles. Realizing beforehand that this may happen is some preparation for the day of its happening.

Naturally, we all wish to retain the most prestigious status that fills our most highly esteemed self-definition. There is nothing wrong with this, nor with the desire to have prominent status in the first place, unless we are motivated by excessive pride or by a desire to stand above others to dominate them.

It's interesting that in 1 Timothy 3:1 when the apostle Paul talks about leadership roles in the church he says, "It is quite true to say that a man who sets his heart on holding office has laudable ambition"

(Phillips). Then the apostle goes on to set forth conditions for qualification. He's saying that it's okay to
want leadership status and roles. Far from denigrat-
ing proper ambition, he simply advises it be kept
within appropriate bounds, properly motivated for
high ends.

Roles: How Statuses Are Acted Out

The way that statuses are acted out are called "roles"
and "role performance." The two are inseparable. Here
we can combine two notions to speak of "status-
induced roles."

The sociologist refers to social roles as "personal
behaviors for fulfilling expectations socially assigned
to different statuses."

As a church pastor (achieved status), my role was
to minister to people in various accepted ways. Later,
as a professor of sociology (successively achieved status), my role was to competently teach certain subjects
to students. Now, as a retired professional (newly
achieved status), my role is to . . . and here the problem developed (I should say dramatically developed!).

Here comes to mind the famous line from William
Shakespeare's *As You Like It*: "All the world's a
stage,/And all the men and women merely players:/They have their exits and their entrances;/And
one man in his time plays many parts . . ." Today,
Shakespeare would say "roles."

Sociologists have long seen the theatrical stage as
a splendid analogy for human social action—people

interacting as social entities, each performing varied and changing roles as actors on the world stage.

So we all take on our particular roles, with role-performance a consequence of social learning. How we fulfill any given role is first learned by observing the interactions of others fulfilling similar roles. We then take on whatever roles we select as appropriate. In daily experience we soon learn the precise congruity expected between statuses and roles. As life situations evolve, we adapt to changing statuses and take on their appropriate roles.

Not by ourselves alone do we learn what our statuses are or the roles appropriate to them but only as we interact in social settings. So we are socialized within those groups where we are participants. Some groups are classified as "formal" (business or university colleagues, political party associates); others as "informal" (family, friendship circles, church fellowship, bowling club).

Within each group setting we are socialized so as to assimilate group values, attitudes, and actions. If we're to establish ourselves as accepted members of the group, we must first accept the group's norms and standards. Then our behavior adapts to them. We learn all the checks and balances, the proper protocol, and then make sure our role-performance is appropriate for our status. In this way we gain the group's approval and share in whatever rewards the group has to offer. Insofar as we may not accommodate to the group norms and standards, we merit disapproval and probable sanctions, even rejection. By failing to perform the roles expected of us, we fail to gain the status of an approved member, thus jeopardizing our place. We gain approval by conformity and lose approval by nonconformity. This applies to membership in all groups, including our occupational group where we find our master-status.

Statuses and Self-Identification

Whether within formal groups or within informal groups, our statuses become central to our self-definition. We perceive ourselves—and think others perceive us—as having a particular status. It is part of our self-image.

It isn't difficult to see how profound an effect statuses and roles have on attitudes and behavior. It was contemporary sociologist, Peter Berger, who first showed that the roles we play not only dictate our actions but transform us in the process. The method known as "role-playing" has been used by the Stanford social psychologist, Philip G. Zimbardo, and others to demonstrate how we create our self-definition out of the roles we play.

How we perceive ourselves has a lot to do with the way we act out our roles. I once had a beloved associate in the ministry. He was a layman, with no training for ministry, but he had great ability to minister to people on a one-to-one basis. He had been a successful sales manager, and despite his lack of formal training for ministry, he considered himself well-equipped. It was both amazing and delightful to see how others saw him as competent in the ministry role.

He projected to others the image he had given himself. He had adopted a certain status, played the role well, and was successful.

In the course of a day, each of us plays various roles. At any one time a particular role is dominant. Entirely separate from my professional role as professor is my private role of husband, say, or my community role as friend or neighbor. As father or grandfather, my role is quite unlike my other roles. The image I project, the language I use, and the behavior I adopt are all adapted to fit the role currently being played within the group where I'm a participant.

That my behavior, like yours, differs in different settings doesn't mean at all that I'm pretending to be someone other than who I really am. Changing roles to fit the setting doesn't make one a chameleon! We need not think something is incongruous about these behaviors. It is not that I'm a mere actor—or hypocrite. You can relax if you've entertained the same questions about yourself. The success with which we play out our roles is a measure of our adaptability to different group settings.

It is simply that there is behavior that is appropriate within one social setting that is quite inappropriate in another. For example, a person conversing with an intimate circle of old friends will be much less formal than when meeting with colleagues in the corporation. In other words, the same person will come across somewhat differently depending on the group of people he's with. In fact, one group might have real difficulty understanding our role-behavior if they were to see us in another group.

Actual Roles versus Envisioned Roles

Some roles are our actual roles—as described above—while others are fantasized roles we'd like to play. Pastor Jack Hayford in his book *Taking Hold of Tomorrow* occasioned some laughter as he pointed to the *Peanuts* cartoon figure Snoopy. Of the many roles Snoopy fantasizes for himself, here is a familiar one as Hayford describes it:

> In adapting to his role as "Joe Cool," Snoopy dons a pair of oversized dark glasses, holds his head at a snobbishly upward tilt, and assumes the air of the sophisticate. He is the worldly-wise man about town, the dog-become-fat-cat who is in touch, in control, on the inside—simply "in."[1]

It doesn't take a Snoopy to be the proficient fantasizer of exotic roles. I confess to my share! Don't we all fit the picture? Generally we fantasize ourselves in some unrealistic or unreachable role, and in our mind we play it out. In that imaginary role we make better decisions than the number-one quarterback in the National Football League, preach better sermons than the most popular preachers, make better policy judgments than the president. We see ourselves as deserving to be pastor of a large, influential church or president of the corporation—a macho type who impresses men and is the debonair man about town in the eyes of women, the impeccable scholar, the internationally known author. Yes, we've all wished for certain statuses and imaginatively played them out in fantasy roles.

Building Statuses

There is great variation in the extent to which preparation early on for one's lifework influences a person's lifestyle. Take the role preparation for physician, lawyer, pastor, or professor. What these roles have in common is their arduous, time-consuming professional training. This involves a long period of education accompanied by a distinct process of professional socialization.

Preparation for a professional career brings young men together who will spend the same number of years in a common course of study and internship. Among them there develops a peer culture and lifestyle that marks them off even from other professions. This socialization provides their identifying badge of belonging; they recognize each other with ease. In this way they are introduced to the importance of specific work-related values, status assignments, and the social roles that mark their particular professional group. They are properly initiated into the "club" with its special prestige, perks, and protocol. Vocational bonding at the higher levels is a powerful unifying force. It establishes self-identity.

Commonly, we say of a profession not our own, "They're a different breed." What we observe is that the status granted professions other than our own is

according to norms and standards unfamiliar to us.
Colleagues in those professions follow their own specific protocol. Men who are initiated into their chosen
profession (internship for doctors, ordination for ministers) begin to build what is called "intrinsic satisfaction" as they act out their roles. By "intrinsic" we
mean work satisfaction that rises from within themselves. That is, personal satisfaction comes from fulfilling a special sense of purpose for which they've
been trained, satisfaction from an attained status, and
ultimately from their record of accomplishment.

This is different from working class men who have
"extrinsic satisfaction"—they gain work gratification
from outside themselves—generally from monetary
rewards or the somewhat private recognition from
within their group workplace.

Occupational Status and Positive Self-Valuation

It is rightly assumed that a man's position in the
status hierarchy is of vital importance to his psychological well-being. How he feels about himself is
directly related to how well his occupational expectations are being fulfilled, including whatever recognition he receives. In other words, a man's overall happiness, whether he is a professional or laborer, is
directly related to how he perceives the value and
rewards of his work—intrinsic or extrinsic. Nonetheless, it seems fair to say that usually it's the professional who has the harder time relinquishing his
work, for the very reason that it represents a career

and because the rewards have been intrinsic and widely recognized.

Usually, at first, retirement roles are unfamiliar and hence uncertain. The cynic says, "The role of the retired person is no longer to possess a role." Not true! It is not that we are dispossessed of master-status or roles; we have to accommodate to an altered status with altered roles.

In pre-retirement days, the status "retired" may have been overly fantasized or unrealistically conceived. The picture in mind was perhaps not exactly inauthentic, just beyond reach, somewhat out of focus—dramatized a bit too much before the time.

When a man begins to realize that he isn't quite so sure what his new status will be and what role expectations go with it, problems arise. When there is a change in master-status, there is the grave possibility of not only role-confusion but of role-conflict. Because the new roles are so different and unfamiliar, they can seem completely out of place, making them extremely difficult to take on.

The roles, especially the master-role, that characterize a full-time occupation are dominant influences in shaping a person's sense of well-being. Vocation and healthy self-image are indeed inseparably related. A healthy self-image affects, in turn, one's physical health. Look at what so frequently happens to men who lose their positions in their organizations. They may literally fall apart.

Men who have been professional problem-solvers all through their careers and who were never free from one challenging series of decisions or another and on whose wise choices whole spheres of action depended, find themselves left with self-doubt when in retirement they find few such challenges. Until they gear up once again and engage themselves in some meaningful enterprise, they genuinely wonder if these self-doubts will ever disappear. It's tough to give up a goal-oriented, task-oriented lifestyle!

No longer is self-worth based on what we've been or done. No longer is our social identity affirmed by relationships we've cultivated in our career world. All that has been dismantled; we are now on what Alex Comfort called "the second trajectory." To make the grade here is going to take a lot of effort all over again—more than we've expended in years.

Occupational Status and Personal Satisfaction

An interesting comparison can be made between professional careers and those in private enterprise. Notoriously, private enterprise pays much higher salaries to their employees than are paid, say, to teachers and pastors, with similar educational preparation. But to some extent, rewards in the ministry or in academic positions compensate for lower incomes. Again, it is the intrinsic satisfaction of being directly helpful in the lives of other people, the sense of being engaged in the human enterprise.

I certainly found this to be true both in the ministry and as a college professor. When I left the pastorate after twenty-seven years, I accepted a lower salary to teach in a Christian college. To me, the prestige of a professorship and the joy of teaching and counseling were adequately compensating in terms of overall job satisfaction and personal well-being. There were benefits that a higher salary couldn't buy: I was happy in what I was doing, felt personally fulfilled by many aspects of the academic role, and found that my status in the eyes of others opened many doors of personal and professional effectiveness beyond the college campus.

High-status occupations afford many advantages, among them a high degree of personal autonomy, prestige, and professional perks. The way is opened for great diversity of life-experiences as well as to associations with interesting people in other professions. Studies conclusively show that the higher the occupational status, the more likely a person is to have positive self-valuation and to enjoy the prominence granted him by others. These satisfactions are relatively unrelated to whatever economic assets he is able (or unable) to accumulate. The problem with intrinsic satisfaction is that it ends at retirement.

Studies by C. Edward Noll and others following him consistently find a high correlation between status and personal satisfaction. Is it any wonder, then, that men in the professions so often find retirement a difficult adjustment because they've had to leave behind the source of those satisfactions? Is it any wonder that businessmen accustomed to being in places of leadership have the same difficult time?

Creating the New Persona

What will take the place of the master-status, with its familiar, prestigious roles and intrinsic satisfactions, when retirement arrives? Repositioning, as discussed in chapter 1, must be undertaken with present resources—no leaning on past self-definition, past experience, past resources. It is here that a man may be overtaken by a temporary or long-term state of ambiguity.

The loss of a master-status and its supporting roles need not lead to idleness or a nonproductive life. Nor do the rewards need be the same or even similar to when one was involved in a career. Experience and skills wait to be reemployed for the fulfillment of personal needs. The self-definition created by a useful, needed life is essential, and the retired person must know that he is still a person of worth and still has a place in society. The Christian must still find ways to minister to other human beings in the name of the Lord.

With improved health care, with illness and chronic disease no longer quite the scourge they once were, there is no reason to discourage new and challenging pursuits. In many urban areas senior center counselors are now equipped to guide these choices. Studies by Milton Coleman and others in the 1980s indicate that those who withdraw from social relationships during retirement are most likely to deteriorate. The important element in activities for the retired is not so much material rewards but the rewards embodied in love, esteem, and approval. For the Christian, ample rewards of this nature await in service opportunities, which churches can offer.

A Harris Associates national poll found that only 2 percent of the American public (8 percent of the elderly) selected sixty years of age or older as the "best years of a person's life." Roughly one-third of both the general public and the elderly selected the sixties and seventies as the "worst years of a person's life." Understandably then, the retirement crisis is burdened with the suspicion that the years ahead will not necessarily be the best ones.

As the graying of America proceeds, it is projected that by the year 2000 there will be nearly 32 million elderly Americans—12.3 percent of the population of the United States. The American Association of Retired Persons estimates that one out of every three people who retire would prefer to continue working. Research studies document that men in retirement are just as likely to increase their involvement in activities and job-related tasks as they are likely to decrease their involvement. What this says is that a large number of retirees want to be utilized in constructive ways. This leads many sociologists to conclude that, in general, professionals and businessmen who remain meaningfully active during retirement will be the best adjusted. It is a need they have within themselves, the continuing need for intrinsic satisfaction.

Jules Willing reminds those of us who are retired that we still work subconsciously to create an acceptable "persona." The stakes now are not as high, and roles are more relaxed and natural, but the presentation of a valued self is still important. Of greatest importance to the Christian should be the presentation of self as authentic and centered in a vital, growing relationship with the Lord.

> Commit everything you do to the Lord. Trust him to help you do it and he will.
>
> [Psalm 37:5 TLB]

3

Profile of a Personal Trauma

My early retirement years, first in San Jose, then in Santa Maria, were a time for celebrating the grand release—the end of obligatory work schedules and new freedom to engage in projects that suited our interests as a couple. These initial interests were, however, but the exciting startup—little more than that—of what appeared a freer, less demanding way of life. A larger challenge lay ahead—to find a completely fulfilling life.

At age 62, I left a much-loved college professorship, preceded by 27 years of happy, fruitful pastorates. This was the base on which my personal self-image had been constructed. As my wife and I settled into retirement, everything seemed well on track. With retirement, my sense of identity had to undergo a radical change, however. As I viewed it, my identity had been reduced to something less than it had been and this loss of roles and statuses, the very essence of my self-identification, was a major loss and caught me totally unprepared.

I, like so many men intensely active throughout professional life, thought that knowing who I was as a person had everything to do with the vocation I'd avidly pursued, that is, with what I did day by day, week by week, year in and year out. Much like my peers in teaching and ministry, my self-image had been based on the understandable goals of a productive life—what it took to be successful in my own eyes and in the eyes of others. In other words, I was achievement oriented.

Oh, I didn't see myself as an ambitious person, and especially in the ministry I had genuinely wished to be a servant of others and not to call attention to my ministry as such. Nonetheless, subconsciously, there had been an only-too-human attempt to make some mark in life. So, having now retired from an active and fulfilling career, one in which I had made at least a little mark, all that remained was my writing—the single occupation I'd brought with me into retirement. Within a year I approached a former colleague at Westmont College. "I need a new research and writing project." His response was, "How about the two of us coauthoring a book?" Thus began a welcome project that would take three years and that would take me to Santa Barbara occasionally, back to the college library, back for enjoyable visits with former faculty friends. While there I could envision myself still functioning in the academic community, no longer removed from all that had been my life. For the most part, however, I was home, ensconced in my office, writing. My life found both center and circumference in that location and in the project at hand. Thus developed a way of life that was hardly satisfying to the social person my professional life had trained me to be.

No longer was I the professor teaching students. No longer the faculty person, departmental member, familiar campus figure. Nor was I back in the pastorate, even though I'd served briefly in a part-time retired capacity in San Jose, which proved to be more than I could manage. We moved to Santa Maria and I enjoyed a greater freedom than I had before, but the relative anonymity that came with a new small city encouraged a further drawing back from the intensive public lifestyle that I had known. Invariably, when needing to refer to myself, I spoke in the past tense, in terms of what I'd formerly been.

Just to be no longer pressingly busy was a great pick-me-up. I relished saying "no" to speaking engagements, seminars, conferences, and even church commitments. We were able to enjoy our children and grandchildren and make good on travel plans, unhampered by encroaching semesters of teaching. More than anything, I looked forward to the possibilities for adult education classes—pursuing new avenues of reading, hobbies, social and cultural interests. Unfortunately, these grand ideas remained largely unrealized. Throughout the ongoing weeks there was to be a growing sense that something vital was lacking. Just what I did not know.

A Delayed Retirement Disorientation

Beneath the surface a problem was steadily growing. I had now become relatively inactive socially. Our interactions were pretty well limited to church on Sundays and to a special couple, Torval and Hilja Torvik, who lived a distance away. Such social isolation was to become overwhelming in a way impossible to have foreseen.

Six years into my retirement, three years after we moved to our second home, I began to question every aspect of my changing roles and altered statuses. *Just who am I (or would I be)? What meaningful occupation should I be engaged in? Is there yet any worthwhile purpose I can fulfill? Must I now come to grips with such a grim reality that I'm really out to pasture and haven't recognized it?*

In the early years of retirement it had never dawned on me that what at first seemed little more than a vague restlessness might suddenly become a real depression. I had not considered the effects of an abruptly diminished life, with its altered set of roles and statuses. It all came as a complete surprise. In subtle, growing ways the diminution of social involvement, the severe lessening of relationships, and a highly restricting occupation brought me to the classic post-retirement disorientation. For me it emerged as a delayed crisis.

My past history evidenced no episodes of psychological disorder, no seriously acute periods of anxiety or depression. Nothing, certainly, that could be called an extraordinary psychological downturn. But then, without warning, there came a series of days and nights during which I was helpless to cope with the most ordinary routines. Such a state can only be described as "a delayed retirement disorientation accompanied by depression and dysfunction."

By dysfunction, I mean an inability to first project and then fulfill normal daily objectives, an inability to simply organize tasks. I was gripped by a life-negating mentality, which I neither understood nor could escape. It certainly was not typical of my usual frame of mind. Present time appeared without purpose, future time without prospect. Life came to a virtual standstill, dominated by a new insecurity and uncertainty. It seemed as though everything were closing in on me. There appeared no way out of my confining surroundings to a larger, freer, more purposeful sphere of living. Later I was to identify this sense of confinement as psychological self-imprisonment, a confinement of spirit largely of my own making. Typical of a sense of depressive entrapment was my acceptance of a narrowed world of thinking and activity. Exacerbating a sense of isolation was an unwitting tendency to turn inward. Drawing an invisible wall around myself, I placed outside of it much that was vital to a continuing flow of stimulating interests and healthy social engagement. I'd witnessed in others such a condition of partial lostness but had never dreamed of experiencing it myself.

We had just returned from two very special visits with pastor friends from seminary days when things seemed to cave in on me. Both friends had retired about the same time as I had. They both were now enjoying serving half-time on church staffs, performing ministries that satisfied their own need to be useful in the Lord's work. Yet each had time to enjoy retirement as well—a beautiful balance! As I compared each man's fulfilled life with the relative unfulfillment of my own, a severe reaction set in. When we returned home after the second visit, I experienced an unusual resistance on walking into our house, especially against going into my study where I'd face that electronic taskmaster to which I'd given obeisance over the past three years. The very walls seemed forbidding. An ominous sense of imprisonment overtook me.

Over a span of eight days—the most trying period of my adult years—there stretched an acute episode of personal depression, disorientation, and severe dysfunction. I'd been retired for six years, seemingly with this new stage of life going quite well. Enough so, at least, to scorn any thought of someday going through a severe crisis that would result in confused self-identity, a questioning of personal worth, and paralysis of activity.

I would awaken to morbid thoughts, with confused pictures of reality and severe nervous tension. Sometimes I awoke in a cold sweat, startled at where I was, still wanting to get out of the house. It was all very irrational, but recognizing the absurdity only added to the problem, for then I felt ashamed and guilty that I was subject to such distortions of reality, that I was so out of touch. It was most troubling to ponder how a mature Christian who had counseled others for years could have such fears and experience such disorientation and depression.

The problem had to do with my perspective being entirely out of kilter. I had lost direction and control. Thankfully, I had not lost awareness of the Lord's grace and goodness, and was still holding strongly to Romans 8:28 (NJKV): "All things work together for good to those who love God, to those who are the called according to His purpose."

For a full week the downturn continued unrelentingly and with increasing severity. Able to sleep only a few hours each night, I would sometimes arise when it was still dark, take my Bible and hymnbook, and seek the Lord's face. I pled with the Lord to deliver me from this darkness of spirit, this absence of direction, this crippling emotional helplessness. Often he met me, but I was still losing the battle overall.

> Come down, O Christ, and help me!
> Reach out Thy hand.
> For I'm drowning in a stormier sea,
> Than Simon on Thy Lake of Galilee!
>
> Oscar Wilde
> *E. Tenebris*

The Rebirth of Hope

Intermittently, through the days of that agonizing week, hopeful moments would return. Classic hymns had a magnificent power to lift me out of myself and into God's presence. In glorious ways he affirmed his omnipotence and faithfulness. It was nothing less than the overriding grace of him whom my faith had so long embraced. When I couldn't pray with my own words, I would pray the words of specific hymns. The glorious vision of God contained therein never failed to lead me upward with affirmations of new liberty in Christ my Lord. Hymns were second only to Scripture in the sustaining strength I received that week. Underneath were the everlasting arms!

Continually the conviction grew that God had his own reasons for permitting this affliction of mind and spirit. For my part, I was beginning to recognize there could be no deliverance until certain lessons had been learned, certain corners turned, certain commitments made. Clearly, there was his part; there was also my part. Growth could not come without first a searching of heart and life, without first releasing all my needs into his hands.

Early on, a journal of those successive days and nights began to take shape. Initially this came about without conscious purpose other than as a continuous reminder of what I was going through, and when and how God was meeting me. Then as time went on, those accumulating insights—the record of God's drawing near—served as powerful testimony to progress being made into the light and strength of his grace. Here was evidence of special times when he did indeed break through with precious assurances. The journal was also a testament to his gift of increasing self-understanding. Most importantly, he let me know repeatedly that he was there—there for me!

As the days multiplied, there were more insights, more assurances, renewed inner strength. Nonetheless, while ongoing progress was real, the process was overwhelmed by a terribly regressive period toward the end of that black week. I began losing the battle.

Early on I found I could not go through this ordeal by myself. As early as 4:30 in the morning I would awaken my wife, Ruth, asking her just to sit, talk, read, and pray with me. Sometimes I could only sob out my feelings of helplessness and try to describe the sense of isolation and darkness surrounding me, what appeared a hopeless future if indeed I were no longer able to be a ministering person. Even though a child of God, I had become filled with irrational fears and morbid thoughts, ashamed and guilt-ridden that these were somehow able to intrude at this late period of my Christian walk.

In her own wonderful way, Ruth was there with me and for me. Shining through was the empathic result of years of companionship. Intuitively, she knew how to facilitate my self-understanding through listening, caring comments, and constant encouragement. What a tower of strength she was!

Little did it dawn on me then how severely this crisis of mine must have touched her spirit with an equal depth of concern. For in the midst of depression, how entirely self-focused one becomes. Every caring spouse in such a circumstance must recognize this and work around it. God has his own gift for ministering spouses!

Now, removed far beyond that fearful week, I look back and know for sure I couldn't have survived this dark period without her support, her steadiness, insights, and prayer. God had surely provided in wonderful ways; she represented the greatest of those ways.

One week into this darkness, I felt compelled to give my friend Torval Torvik an early morning call. I needed his ministry as a pastor and a friend at once. From my rather broken speech with its emotional overtones, he could readily sense the need was critical. With a pastor's intuition, he and his wife went to prayer for me. Soon after breakfast Ruth and I were on our way to see them.

Wisely the two wives left us for most of the day. For T. G. and me it was a blessed time of deep relating, a time washed with tears and lifted by prayer, infused with unspoken mutual understanding and empathy. Together we stood upon God's Word, as the Spirit of God brought relevant promises to mind. In such an hour, how blessed indeed to have the strong touch of a mature, spiritual friend!

Is any support greater than that of dear ones, family or friends, who can stand with us and be part of the battle? Make no mistake; they too suffer with us. But when victory comes, theirs is also a share in the rejoicing. Is this not the mutual burden-bearing of which the New Testament speaks? How true the word of Jesus that burdens become lighter when laid upon him, and when there are others to share them.

It was the eighth day of personal wandering, but that day spent with T. G. was the turning point. Beyond all doubt, I knew it! The clouds broke and the sun shone—literally and emotionally! Within a few days I was back to normal inner health and with new-found self-understanding. God had met and touched me. Deeply meaningful lessons were falling into place. To hear what he was saying, to see what he was doing, was encouraging. Even exciting.

Finally the Lord's use of a pastor and those close to me proved sufficient to draw me out of my depressed state. Different individuals must be helped in different ways and at times a therapist's intervention will be necessary.

God's gift of self-understanding brought me a rather swift and complete reorientation both in direction and in the health that goes with it. Soon I was back to rational thinking and positive, hopeful expectations. With clearer thinking and a sense of God's gracious intervention came the return to stabilized emotions and social involvement. Best of all, I could look ahead, not just behind. Life did indeed have a prospect.

Over the next two months only a few minor setbacks dogged my steps, then full recovery. Best of all, throughout the recovery period, I knew the battle was over, the victory won. I simply had to lay hold of it, then live out its reality, as God measured out strength and guidance on a day-to-day basis.

There was, indeed, hope for a fulfilling life ahead! Perhaps more in growing than in doing. His proposition was one which only faith could grasp. But, too, I had to release the reins of control. Obedience required letting him take greater control, trusting him in the dark as in the light.

At just the right juncture, Ruth said, "The Lord's given me a verse for you, Jeremiah 29:11, 'For I know the plans I have for you, says the Lord, plans for good and not for evil, to give you a future and a hope.'" She added, "You see how nothing in that promise points to the past; the past is no longer the relevant thing."

So together Ruth and I claimed this promise for ourselves. There was a future and a hope! Indeed! It lay in God's sovereign will! I could trust him, yes, could rest at peace in his will! No longer was there a place for self-assertive, anxious planning on my own.

Insights Gained

My Personal Crisis	Application
Relocation to a city where we didn't know people after 2½ years into retirement.	A major geographical move with no waiting associations are serious stress factors.
Ruth's day remained pretty much the same. My daily pattern was completely different.	What meets the needs of one member of a couple may not meet the needs of the other.

Insights Gained (cont.)

My Personal Crisis	Application
Unsettled church and social relationships.	A church family is vital to the process of resocialization.
Post-retirement disorientation was caused when circumstances led to identity loss without compensating gains.	When there is major-status loss, there must be compensating gains, which have been prepared for in advance.
My status, roles, and identity were all radically altered at one fell swoop.	Self-definition is dependent on some continuity of statuses, roles, and relationships. An abrupt alteration can be devastating.
I was an occupationally displaced person.	A major occupational displacement will always have a destabilizing effect on everything else, including spousal contentment.
I had to ask "Who am I?" "What is my present self-definition?" "Am I still needed?"	Every retiree can expect these questions. They ought to be resolved before retirement through retirement counseling.
Disorientation, depression, and dysfunction followed in close succession.	Dysfunction will follow a depressive reaction. It need not last long if proper steps are taken.

Insights Gained (cont.)

My Personal Crisis	Application
I was plagued with thoughts of having failed God and that he would no longer use me.	When we submit ourselves to him, he always has plans for us.
My focus was on productivity rather than personal growth. When I was no longer doing, I wondered where I fit in the scheme of things.	Renewed faith is the key: faith that we have "place" with him.
I found solace in Scripture, especially in the Psalms and the promises of God's abiding presence and help.	David echoes the same questions that we have and provides answers applicable to men in all times.
My knowledge of God's promises hadn't been tested in the crucible.	Truth must be experienced for it to be truth for us. God permits our struggle if it leads us to a deeper understanding and a deeper walk.
With confession, simply placing myself before the Lord as one undone, I discovered myself joining the everlasting testimony that, yes, he hears our cries and answers.	When we turn our defeats into contrite submission to him, he enables us to rise with new assurance that he will not leave us in darkness, doubt, and defeat.

Insights Gained (cont.)

My Personal Crisis	Application
I questioned whether I could ever be used again in God's service.	God has a special place of usefulness for each one. It isn't our gifts, but the one who gifts us.
Was I nursing a selfish reluctance to serve God because I felt my own needs were not being met as I thought they should be?—a dangerous attitude for a supposedly mature Christian!	We must assume proper responsibility for our own lives and not blame God for our unhappiness and frustrations.
We were unable to find a new church home that was exactly what we were seeking. I was critical of the church we attended.	To refuse to allow God to order his local church as he sees best is an affront to him who calls us to fit in with his enabling and to rejoice in what he's doing, however unfulfilled our traditions may remain.
I sought to live in the past, finding my value and fulfillment there.	We must be disciplined to let go and move on, keeping the present as the true reality. God calls us to give our best to gain the most with what is left.

4

Losses
Don't Make Losers

In her book *Necessary Losses*, Judith Viorst provides an excellent summary of one of the major elements contributing to the problem tackled in this book: "Work shores up our identity; it anchors both the private and social self; it defines that self to itself and to the world. And lacking a workplace to go to, a circle of colleagues to connect with, a task to confirm our competence, a salary that puts a value on that competence, a job description that serves as a shorthand way of telling strangers who we are, we may—when we have retired—start to ask, with growing anxiety, 'Who am I?'"[1]

Viorst's words perfectly describe the combination of conditions that lay behind my own coming to the place of asking "Who am I?"

There is no question that for many men retirement can best be generalized as loss. Whatever gains eventually come out of it, the transition is initially marked by enormous loss, especially position, status, work roles. Like many other life changes, it is essentially loss of control over one's life in some major fashion. And to the degree control has become a strong value attached to one's self-identification, such loss is bound to be severe. Thus, the degree to which one's vocational position has afforded control, the greater the sense of loss. Moreover, retirement means loss of colleagues, even associations reaching far beyond the workplace itself. Add daily routines, deadlines, team projects, even the office itself where one feels comfortable amid familiar material surroundings. We so unthinkingly take for granted the very physical surroundings we live with daily—opening the same door in the morning, locking it in the afternoon. Ah, yes, even the restroom down the hallway!

Take the loss of one's rank in the organization's pecking order, or the way the hours of the day and days of the week are organized and lived out in a self-repeating pattern. It's all part of the overall loss of place and self-definition that occurs so suddenly with retirement. It isn't that one's self-image is distorted; it's shattered!

Losing, Leaving, Letting Go

With any major loss we feel personally diminished, thus never quite the same person we were. With each loss, we acknowledge with our mind that something's irretrievable, but the rest of us goes on trying to deny the fact. As Viorst continues: "We live by losing and leaving and letting go. And sooner or later, with more or less pain, we all must come to know that loss is indeed a lifelong human condition."[2]

In her closing pages, Viorst sums it up: "Losing is the price we pay for living. It is also the source of much of our growth and gain. Making our way from birth to death, we also have to make our way through the pain of giving up and giving up and giving up. . . . We have to deal with our necessary losses. . . . And in confronting the many losses that are brought by time and death, we become a mourning and adapting self, finding at every stage—until we draw our final breath— opportunities for creative transformations."[3] This says it all.

Add up the important elements:

1. Loss is inevitably a part of all living.
2. The pain of loss cannot be denied.
3. Anger and resentment, however valid, must be relinquished as quickly as possible.
4. Loss must be dealt with forthrightly if we are to survive and move on.
5. Grieving for major loss must be given time.
6. The challenge of loss is to creatively turn negatives into positives.

It needs to be driven home not only as truth but as our truth—your truth, my truth! Then we can acknowledge that since life is a continuation of adapting to loss, each of us needs to become "an adapting self."

As Viorst depicts it, "an adapting self" must first become "a grieving self" if there is to be a positive strategy for coping. Adapting incorporates grieving as its first step.

Contrary to common assumptions, grieving is not an altogether negative experience any more than loss itself. And when grieving is completed, it moves us beyond negatives to positive loss-resolution, and then opens us to purposeful living. Grieving, in its completion, brings about a change in both fundamental attitude and direction, integrating the emotional and the practical in a new and positive mind-set.

As the James and Cherry *Grief Recovery Handbook* has it, "Simply put, grief is a normal and natural response to loss. . . . We grieve for the loss of all relationships that could be held as significant and therefore emotional. . . ."[4] In other words, loss of anything that has major importance—a person, relationship, attachment, any loss that brings emotional distress and the sense of personal diminution—is cause for grieving, and grieving must run its course unimpeded.

There is another side. If loss is meant to be a means to ultimate gain, then to eventually be unable to let go and move on is pathological grieving. It is possible to grieve one's way straight to a psychological dead end.

The observation of these grief recovery experts is sound: "Since almost everything we've learned is about what we can acquire in order to feel complete or whole, the process of losing something feels wrong, unnatural, or broken."[5]

Is it any wonder, they ask, that loss so commonly prompts little more than negative responses? We look back, wishing things could be (a) different, (b) more, (c) better, (d) unchanging, (e) repeatable. We wish something or someone were still here. We feel deprived of the person or thing that would bring us success or happiness. Now we must continue the journey toward completeness and wholeness with no chance of success. How unnecessarily we pile nonessential baggage onto our grieving! These inappropriate thoughts only succeed in preventing what could be positive results.

Steps in the Grieving Process

From the first writing of Elisabeth Kübler-Ross, health care experts have assumed that there are specific steps in the grieving process, that grieving always follows the same pattern. That is, the bereaved person experiences shock, distress, depression, anger, denial, blame. There has been an established assumption that a patterned progression of grief-steps is necessary, a progression that proceeds from inability to perceive and cope realistically to an eventual acceptance and adaptation, at which point positive functioning resumes once again. Any real ability to function well doesn't come about until certain steps are completed in a certain order.

But is this always the case? Is each of these steps necessary? Do they always follow in order? This is widely questioned today.

According to Camille Wortman and Roxanne Silver of the University of Michigan, who've studied what they call "the myths of coping with loss," people don't always conform to a fixed pattern. Our society is critical of those who grieve. If someone doesn't grieve openly and considerably, the experts categorize this as "denial." If there is prolonged grieving, this is categorized as "morbid" or "self-indulgent." Judgments such as these are often seriously in error.

Grieving Follows Individual Patterns

What these authorities take pains to point out is that there are no definitions for "normal" grieving or for "working through." At the beginning of the '90s, too little is known as yet about the full spectrum of grieving to claim that a single pattern fits all people. Today, this is quite generally conceded.

Grieving is a personal and individual process. For one thing, people differ in the emotional responses they bring to a major loss. An individual's background and other factors prepare him or her for the grieving response. The nature of the loss, how it's interpreted, the maturity and personal resources of the person suffering the loss all contribute to an individual pattern of grieving and route to recovery.

All this is important for Christian men and women to understand, considering the ways in which God meets differing experiences of loss together with differing grief and recovery processes. God has no set pattern. Rather, he individualizes the recovery plan for each person. Instead of placing everyone in the same category, he brings his loving care to bear uniquely on each of his children.

As severe as grieving invariably proves to be, we can be assured of this—it too comes to an end. Or shall we say, there is an end to which it normally comes. For as Viorst observes, "a time will have to come when we become willing to let go of the lost relationship [our career position in the world, a cherished person through death or divorce, a circle of close friends, or whatever]. Our mourning is pathological when we cannot, and we will not, let it go."[6]

Grieving in Retirement

We usually think of grief as a response to the death of a loved one, but the pain of loss extends through a broad range of experiences in every transition adults pass through, including retirement. Adjusting to each loss follows the same pattern of leaving, losing, and letting go. In whatever area of life they occur, traumatic losses are mourned, and when personal relationships that have extended over years are severed— as they are in retirement—the sense of loss is intense. This kind of loss affects an individual's whole established pattern of living. In retirement more is involved than one's occupation; a whole way of life is altered.

When I was going through my own crisis, I wasn't aware of this. I was struggling with loss far more complex than I realized, and this kind of loss is not amenable to simple solutions. I searched for some elusive single clue to what was happening to me, but there was none.

What is progressively devastating is finding that in every major loss something of our very selves is lost. Abstractly, much of this has to do with our earlier self-definitions, the images we've held of ourselves. How broadly related is this? Self-definition incorporates even such things as physical appearance, attractiveness to others, and acceptance by them. Of course, it includes statuses we assign ourselves and statuses assigned to us by others. Subconsciously, what's important is how, where, and with whom we project our best self-image. The presentation of self, to use Irving Goffman's term, is everything. To our self-image an ever-enhanced complex of qualities is attached.

It's not inconsequential that we speak of "midlife crisis." Here as never before we are conscious of great changes, especially the loss of our younger self—the only self-definition we'd really known thoroughly and counted on to never change.

Midlife changes sound a warning. For one thing, physical changes in the forties are unmistakable and irreversible. As a pastor friend in his late thirties said recently, "I recognize that I'm no longer able to play a game of softball one day and walk the next!" Another observes, "I've exchanged weight lifting for weight watching, jogging for walking."

By the time we reach our fifties each activity is up for reassessment. Whatever takes effort is reconsidered. There's a slowing down, a looking for ways to reduce demands and energy outlays. Means are being sought to end the rat race, to back off and relax a bit more. Stress is catching up. We're looking for short-cuts and hearing warnings from the doctor. We talk about burnout.

So part of the crisis of retirement is aging ("old age is what you're stuck with if you want a long life"). Shocking is the realization that aging no longer refers only to our parents, but to us! We're the aging ones!

As a part of these changes, the compulsive drive that marked our business or professional develop-ment begins to lessen. Ambition notably recedes, and we notice achievement goals slipping from our grasp and expectations undergoing readjustment. It is dis-turbing. Then comes the realization that not every-thing was worth the effort we previously thought. The very nature of reward itself is changing.

One would think that having suffered through a cluster of losses in midlife, we'd be prepared for those that come in the retirement transition. It doesn't seem to operate that way.

Recovery

The greater one interprets any given loss to be, the more traumatic the aftershocks. The positive side, says Viorst, is this: "Through mourning we come to accept the difficult changes that loss must bring—and then we begin to come to the end of mourning."[7] Yes, typi-cally, there is an end point to mourning! Happily, for most people, recovery does come, although more completely and positively for some than for others.

As James and Cherry point out, recovery consists in claiming control of one's circumstances instead of letting circumstances claim us.

Complete recovery is determined by a variety of conditions, most of them resident within the individual's own personality, not in external circumstances. For instance, recovery moves toward completion when memories once again can be enjoyed, when reminiscence no longer precipitates unbearably painful feelings of deprivation or remorse, and when there no longer remains a compulsion to cling unrealistically to the past.

A good recovery allows one to freely acknowledge that it's perfectly okay to look back, to talk negatively about one's losses—even once in a while to feel less than fully recovered. Importantly, the depressive crisis is no longer a bugaboo. We're reminded again—reality never need be denied or repressed. It's all part of normal experience and in no way signals a setback.

James and Cherry locate the final ascent to recovery at the point where the individual realizes that talking about his loss helps others get through theirs. Sharing is a vital part of recovery, a positive consequence of suffering loss. It is the point at which loss's positive features can take dominance. Retired professionals need the kind of supporting people with whom they can share their experience and in the process sense the commonality of what is transpiring in their lives.

I can vouch for this. My own path to full recovery was lighted with bright new assurance when I found myself impelled to share the experience with retired professional friends, many of them pastors. Rather quickly this sharing became a perfectly comfortable thing to do. Through sharing my thoughts and aims, they in turn were consolidated and strengthened.

The act of sharing is itself a wonderfully freeing action, something I soon came to look forward to. I was pleased to pass along that "good thing" God was doing! By now, loss had been transformed into gain!

Along the way I found that listeners had a fascination with how I had come through. Oh, indeed, at first a few were unwilling to disclose their own fears and struggles. As the subject was brought out and discussed in terms of my own experience, typically there came a flood of questions and an acknowledging of concern for themselves. The concern, you can be sure, is out there; I merely tapped into it. A recent seminar I conducted at a retirement facility amply confirmed this need among other retirees.

Reactive Depression

John Bowlby, British psychiatrist and child development authority, in three volumes entitled *Attachment and Loss*, reported in 1980 the active role of loss in relation to depression. He cites, among others, the studies of G. W. Brown, T. Harris, and J. R. Copeland who claim that "loss and disappointment are the central features of most events bringing about clinical depression. While these loss-events are for the most part those such as death, a child leaving for a distant place, or marital breakdown, still some 20 percent were of the nature of a job loss or move to retirement."[8]

Another investigator, Eugene Paykel, found that two-thirds of the events preceding the onset of depressive illness could be classified as losses. Thus, when we consider the depressive reaction suffered in retirement, we're on solid scientific ground. Retirees are not unique in experiencing reactive depression, needing to understand and cope with continued loss.

This connection has caught the attention of contemporary Christian psychologists. Archibald Hart, director of clinical training at the Graduate School of Psychology at Fuller Theological Seminary, in a chapter entitled "Depression as a Response to Loss," writes "I believe that the key to understanding nearly all of the reactive depressions is to see them as a response to a sense of loss."[9]

Hart distinguishes reactive from neurotic depression. His concern is not with the pervasive state of depression rooted in deep-seated anxiety or alienation, nor with biologically related depression. Reactive depression is not treated by medication, but generally by therapeutic counseling, seeking to understand the social conditions that brought about the depressive reaction. If possible, these conditions require changing. At the very least they are to be accepted, then coping measures put into place.

Important to our personal progress is understanding that it is not loss itself but our interpretation of loss that brings depression. This is why different people react differently to the same loss. What we

want depression to accurately reflect is the true significance of the loss, not some distortion. Then we can
deal realistically with it. In this way depression serves
a valuable function—as Hart and the grief recovery
experts add—if the depression is not excessively prolonged.

Curiously, while the natural tendency is to deny
depressive states a legitimate place, depression is
intended to serve a healthy function. For one thing,
pain brought on by depression registers the magnitude of the problem, calling attention to the urgent
need to deal with it. The depressed individual is urged
on toward a positive, pain-relieving resolution. There
are only two alternative outcomes: either the suffering person will sink deeper into the depression or
move on to recovery.

In retrospect, I see my own depressive experience
as serving a healthy function. Not that I could have
predicted this result at the time. Gripping, agonizing
depression, with its confused and hopeless intro
spection, was all part of the shock of loss, the mourning of loss, and having to endure a process I'd otherwise have sought to avoid. In a crucial way, it brought
to my attention just how deeply I interpreted the loss
of statuses, roles, and associations, and how severe
were the costs in mental and emotional pain.

Of loss itself there are several forms. Our concern is
with what is called "abstract loss," the loss of intangibles. On the one hand we have loss of a job, an office,
associates, children leaving home, a spouse—these are
tangible losses. On the other hand, loss of love, hope,

status—intangibles such as these—are losses in the abstract. These are among the less easily recognized losses because we are unable to point concretely to a loss-object. These are subjective, not objective losses. But they become part of our growing "loss account."

Hart concurs that grief is the appropriate response to loss, describing the grief process in ways similar to those we've looked at. As all loss is subject to the grieving process, not the least notable are these abstract losses.

Take hope as an example. Loss of hope can result from inability to perceive a future for oneself, from real or imagined personal rejection or disconnection. The future seems shut off from oneself. We lose hope in ourselves, in other people, in the very events we're caught up in. Does our hope in God's providence become shaken? Sometimes. Usually transiently.

Take another example—the loss felt when one is no longer a prominent person, or no longer greatly needed, out of the public eye. For retired people, this abstract loss is sometimes experienced without being understood as such. This is the specter of retirement loss. In my own experience there was a special, nagging sense of opportunities forever gone, a longing to make up for failures accumulated along life's way. But all second chances seemed gone; it no longer appeared possible to re-engage the multitude of opportunities long since gone by the boards. This only exacerbated feelings of hopelessness.

Of course, we all have regrets over past failures; none of us differs in this regard. To any thoughtful older Christian, at some point or another this brings pain. The more critical time to expect such regrets is retirement when we have greater occasion to reflect on the past. The failures of former years now appear luminous and more than a little exaggerated.

How easily we're led to dwell on lost opportunities, magnifying past occasions when we might have exerted some helpful effort but didn't, might have committed ourselves to others' needs but didn't, might have witnessed for the Lord, but didn't. Now that those opportunities are no longer ours to pursue, failure through omission looms more significant than ever before. Especially for those who've been in places of public ministry, conscience tends to render an accusatory inner accounting. But we cannot flagellate ourselves. We must accept the fact that opportunities once ours are for the most part past and gone. We can't live by regrets. God doesn't ask it of us. We can only work with what we have. We can make the best of what is left.

Couple this with feelings that reduced activity may be interpreted by others as indolence—a further wasting of opportunities to be useful ("servants of God, faithful to the end, dying with our boots on"). Since a sense of God's call to ministry never vacates the pastor-heart, remorse over failures of ministry only exacerbates guilt feelings among those of us coming from this serving background. Pastors' high self-expectations produce enough guilt as it is. This feature is not so prominent with men retiring from business or the other professions.

Many professionals tend to be perfectionists, probably trying to live up to the adulation they've received over the years (authenticating their press reviews!). But to look at life as it was before retirement is, from a perfectionist's viewpoint, to see most of the past as a sad chronicle of failures large and small. This is something professionals tend to do, and do so regardless of career successes. Now they tend to see retirement as "the last chance" to rectify past mistakes.

"How," one agonizes, "is it possible to relax and even be a little self-indulgent when there's so much to make up for?" But this is the prompting of a conscience that cannot accept the realities of human imperfection. Again, it places what we do (and do not do) above who and what we are as struggling fellow travelers in an imperfect world. Sadly, a mind-set like this effectively keeps us from letting go and moving on.

Compulsions of this kind disregard such realities as the growing limitations of health and energy. There is diminished capacity to grasp opportunities that are always "out there." Now, even as before, occasions for ministry are going to come, only to go by the board. We, especially, who so long were in positions of ministry need to settle it once and for all that personal limitations are going to be with us from now on.

There is undoubtedly a nearly universal sense of loss that accompanies the knowledge of having lived at less than our absolute best. Although generally a matter of over-sensitivity, this regret must be dealt with like any other loss. In most instances, time will bring acceptance of the imperfect past with its failures and lost opportunities, and we'll stop struggling with it.

For Christians, this sensitivity to our imperfect past needs to be committed to God's forgiving grace. As forgiven persons, we're to forgive ourselves and live in the reality of our forgiveness. When we do, we're relieved of the compulsion to strive unduly to "make up" what cannot be made up. What we can be assured of is that there are still opportunities to be grasped. We can commit ourselves once more to attempting our best, not with the thought that such efforts make up for past failures, but for this end alone.

Another abstract loss that goes with retirement is the loss of dreams. For example, one couple has dreamed of having a summer cottage or recreational vehicle. But now retired, insufficient financial assets prevent the dream from becoming reality.

For another couple time now allows for travel never before possible, but decreasing health doesn't permit it.

Still another couple has long dreamed of being free to locate near their children. But now the children do not seem keen for the idea, and friends advise against it. All plans come to a halt. Dreams turn to disillusionment.

Then there are dreams cut short by the death of a spouse. Whether it's money, circumstances, health, death—each has a way of turning dreams to ashes. The loss side of the ledger is lengthening.

For me, retirement was not something I viewed at first as an enormous adjustment. Sure, there were losses that couldn't easily be dismissed. But the future, while still vaguely perceived, surely seemed promising. Although I didn't realize it, there had to follow, sooner or later, a grieving and recovery process. Had I not suffered a depressive episode of such magnitude well into retirement, the need for grieving and recovery might not have been recognized at all. If early on, the full sense of loss had been suppressed, there would surely have been damage—possibly irreparable damage.

So if you, my reader, are undergoing a depressive state because of major losses, take heart. The depressive state can serve a positive purpose. Be assured of this, having accomplished its gainful end, the pain will pass. Patiently go on, making allowance for whatever steps are needed in your own particular case.

Remember, only losers let losses make them losers! Losses themselves can't make losers!

5

No Longer Shackled to the Past

Why are we prone to look back, seek to relive our past, let what was back then stand in the way of what is now? Why are we drawn so compulsively toward trying to recapture a life now gone? What is so seductive about those years that no longer exist except in fond reminiscence?

Let's take a stab at some answers.

First, the past is all we know for certain; it's already ours by experience; we possess it. The present is still tentative while the future is altogether unknown. Neither present nor future are yet a part of our living history. We find security as well as self-identification in clinging to that which cannot change. Our ever-changing life needs secure underpinnings, and our past provides that for us. We are secure in what we know for sure.

Second, in part, we are captives to nostalgia for what we've loved and lost or left behind—long-familiar neighborhoods, close friends, loved ones, a significant career, meaningful social circles, fulfilling activities, statuses gained along the way, multiple roles played— all the people, events, and involvements that are part of a fairly long lifetime. This aura of nostalgic reminiscence is created by emotional attachments to the past.

A distinction here should prove helpful. Reminiscence is the process of recalling past events. Nostalgia is an affective component that sometimes but not always accompanies reminiscence. While related, the two are distinct. Reminiscence is spontaneous recall, useful in our sustaining an overall inventory of mental images attached to the history of the self. As one prominent psychiatrist explains it, "By monitoring the process of change that inevitably occurs over time, reminiscence contributes in a fundamental way to the stability and integrity of the personality."[1] This point we shall return to.

Originally the word *nostalgia* meant homesickness—the painful longing for joys attached to places and persons now removed. The word comes from the Greek term meaning "to return home." Curiously it also carries the sense of being a painful condition. In the evolving etymology, the word came to mean that which a person longs for that belongs to another time—usually past, sometimes future.

Nostalgia is generally regressive in that it shuns the present. When nostalgia stays within the bounds of reality and is not compulsive it is perfectly normal. The problem with nostalgia is the way it blows things out of proportion, idealizes beyond reality, and adds an exaggerated emotional component to the object of reminiscence. It is true that many retirees struggle against a compulsive nostalgia bonded to what has been lost or left behind. This nostalgia drives them to seek recovery of the past. The retiree who lives too largely and unrealistically in reminiscence has moved toward pathological nostalgia.

Third, each of us is the living product of past experiences; we are our social history. To know ourselves as unique individuals, different from all others—to have our own self-definition—is to see ourselves in the sweeping panorama of our unique social history. We cannot detach ourselves from that history.

Inescapably, people and events, now filed away in memory, form the content of our personal history. They form the record of how we've come to be the people we are, and the continuity of past and present validates who we are. To relive these memories is to keep alive all the elements that contributed toward making us the human products we've become. What we are is of importance only as it relates to what we're becoming. What we're becoming extends into the future, and of that we know nothing for certain. Thus our "becoming" attaches most significantly to what we have been.

So, then, the past is forever concretely deposited in our personalities and cannot be dislodged. In this history of our lives, this extended narrative of the years, indelibly written in memory and open to reminiscence, we see our true selves—the lengthened shadows of all the changes that make up that history. At any given moment, the meaning of a life is the sum of all the meanings processed up to that point.

Jules Willing summarizes the problem that is faced at retirement: "We have spent all our working lives creating our own personal history, our eyes fixed on the future consequences of our acts and decisions. There has always been a next stage in our careers, the events of which we are formulating in the present. . . . But now for the first time we have reached the place where our history stops; there is no next stage. . . . For the first time, we can measure the entire distance from where we started a lifetime ago to the farthest place we have reached."[2]

Clearly, we see that memory of the past cannot be dissociated from the ability to live coherent lives over time. Living out the present is simply extending what we've been becoming throughout the entirety of our personal history. Thus is our identity continually formed through the whole of life.

Timothy K. Jones, in a splendid article in *Christianity Today* aptly titled "Reading Life Backwards," speaks of our need for a continuous inner narrative—knowing where we've been in order to know who we are. He affirms, "We need not lose sight of the turns, twists, and detours that have brought us to the present." Then he follows with a quote from Frederick Buechner's self-analysis: "My interest in the past is not, I think, primarily nostalgic. Like everybody else, I rejoice in much of it and marvel at those moments when, less by effort than by grace, it comes to life again with extraordinary power and immediacy. . . . But what quickens my pulse now is the stretch ahead rather than the one behind, and it is mainly for some clue to where I am going that I search through where I have been, for some hint as to who I am becoming or failing to become that I delve into what used to be."[3]

The Best Time of My Life

Reminiscing is, of course, never truly objective (nostalgic reminiscence less so!) but is rather a subjective exercise. Our past is modified as memory creatively rewrites it, for memory is both selective and creative, having a genius for transforming the actual past into an idealized, more desirable past. As someone said, "And so we readily pass from autobiography to novel." Mentally, we reconstruct the past so as to construe it in its best light. Thus the "good old days," "fantastic places," and "great events" are all richly colored by memory's creative genius. Selectively, we remember most vividly what we wish—or need—to remember—for the most part what was good and pleasant.

As memory crafts a new past out of the old by making it appear better, nothing within us protests the reconstruction. Giving us what we wish, we then rehearse it over and over, each new telling of it sounding more authentic than the one before! In no time at all we have a past marvelously transmuted into an "official" version—one well worth reciting!

Aging, someone remarked, is "when we experience fewer and fewer things for the first time, more and more things for the last time." We find pleasure in remembering all we've experienced in the past, especially now that present experiences are diminishing.

Aging, as another put it, is "when the sum total of our memories exceeds the sum total of our hopes." Disconcertingly, the future is being inexorably shortened, life's end point coming more clearly into view. As future prospects become less pronounced, the past becomes more pronounced. It crowds our minds and calls for attention because the past is what we can be most sure of.

Thus, while the past is no longer a living, present reality, it provides the necessary continuity to the narrative-making of one's life. Once concrete realities—who we've been, what we've done, where we've lived, worked, and worshiped, and the people with whom our lives have been intertwined—formed us into the unique people that we are. It's impossible for a person to be anything other than that which has been developing all along. At this moment, he occupies a point in the long continuum that marks the progressive development of the self from birth to present. So remembrance of the past is highly important! Pity the one with Alzheimer's disease who has lost all memory of the past; there is no longer a means of knowing one's self.

Among the illuminating books to come into my hands is the classic work of Simone de Beauvoir, *The Coming of Age*. She asks why older people keep summoning up images of the past, and remarks, "They are not trying to make a detailed, coherent account of their earlier years, but rather to plunge back into them. Again and again they turn over a few themes of great emotional value to them; and far from growing tired of this perpetual repetition, they return to it with even greater pleasure. They escape from the present; they dream of former happiness; they exorcise past misfortunes."[4]

I'm sure that at one time or another all of us see in ourselves this compulsion to look back rather wistfully, to try reliving some aspect of what once was our lot. We regress to wishful thinking about a supposedly uncomplicated youth or about some previous period now idealized as "the best time of my life." For retired professional men, this period usually embraces the years of vocational challenges—hard work and reward—the years totally invested in a career, now seen in a rosy light.

Looking back is frequently a coping mechanism, a diversion, promising deliverance from unmanageable circumstances now menacing us. Dwelling on some former period in our personal history can make the past take on greater attractiveness than the present for which the former was exchanged. Generally the retired professional's or businessman's reminiscence concentrates on former close associations in "the organization." One is mentally trans-

ported back to the past, once again in lively conversation with "the guys," for these were times they
thought they had it all together, when things were
more secure, when a carefully thought-out future
pulled them forward.

Of course, memories that compel our looking back
are by no means limited to fond ones. There are deep
hurts, unremitting guilts, sometimes haunting unre-
quited loves. Our minds sometimes seem shackled
to painful, alienated relationships and to people
whose forgiveness we need (or who stand in need of
our forgiveness). Often it's this kind of unfinished
business that draws our minds back, driving us to
rethink the courses we've taken. Especially difficult
are the "if only's."

What is difficult for us to grasp is that however cruel
life's negations have been, however dark the deeds
we've done—or have had done to us—the only continuing claim those remembrances can make on us is
that which we permit. Of course, if confession of an
offense can still be made to the offended party, forgiveness asked, restitution made, then memory may
serve to prompt us to beneficial action. But much of
the negative past can only be placed under the forgiveness of God. It's not possible for us to re-create
the past so as to be able to actually deal with it as we
now wish.

Whenever, say, some dark specter out of the past
gives birth to a bitter, unforgiving spirit, prayer for
release and cleansing is the sure antidote. To bring
these matters up again and again is to deny the for-

giveness God has already put in place. Furthermore, it is failing to lay hold of the victory that Christ offers, a victory that needs only to be appropriated. We do what is still possible, then leave the rest with the Lord and ask him to help us put it out of mind.

With deepening understanding, we see how our own past history—so much of it indelibly etched on memory—invites either sweet nostalgia or dark regret. Either of these evokes a compelling need to reminisce, to engage in a moral review, which continually seeks an assured verdict. Reminiscence promises better understanding and a more constructive dealing with our history, but the effort is often futile, counter-productive, and self-defeating. It's too late.

The question arises: How can I recall the past I've left, with its important role in my overall self-definition, and then let it go in order to move on?

Looking back and hanging on—yes, most of us do this far more proficiently than letting go and moving on. If it seems natural to return to what was then, and it is, then how easily we are seduced away from what is now or what might be! If the natural tendency to look back is allowed to get the better of us, to preclude our getting on with life, then we start acting as though living were indeed behind us altogether.

The Past as Enemy of the Present

This temptation to focus on the past is a problem that tends to surface at the point of any major adult transition. For instance, it arises with loss of health, position, marriage, a loved one—at any point of great change. Its impact is never felt more potently than after we've retired from an active life.

So often some present association triggers the "reminiscence-plus-nostalgia" event. Before we know it, we have a vivid memory of something long repressed—a person, group, place, or series of events. Unbidden, visions spring out of nowhere. For a brief moment, and with no apparent reason, some little scene from the past shines brightly and rivets the attention. Then, as abruptly as it appeared, the vision fades and is lost again. But momentarily it is a fixation, something so powerful, so compelling, as to disable us from embracing the present with its demands, its opportunities, its responsibilities. In most cases, for just a few moments, we are effectively immobilized by the past, but sometimes that immobilization may linger on far longer than the memory that prompted it.

What shall we say? Can the past—so often the friend of the present—become the enemy of the present? It need not, but it often does. More damaging still, other problems and perplexities may be exacerbated when we allow an obsessive preoccupation with the past to take so firm a grip. The present is then indeed crippled by the past.

Unfortunately, though we may know all this about ourselves, unless we are hopeful about the future, have a will to move on, and have a solid trust that God has something better down the road, our discernment will not prevent our inflicting a lot of damage to ourselves.

Helpful Strategies

Discipline yourself to concentrate on what is now. Put aside what was then when you sense it is dominating your thoughts and emotions. You must make an effort to concentrate on what is now. Simple as it may sound, this is never easy! Self-discipline is necessary when we come through any major change in which some significant loss is suffered. This is especially true at retirement, when self-worth is no longer organized around, and supported by, occupational objectives and associations and when we are no longer task-oriented and driven by organizational agendas.

Recognize that memories of a blissful, secure past are an illusion. The connection is apparent: When our daily routine adjusts to the slower pace of retirement, then are we most easily seduced into turning our vision back to the past. Experiencing new insecurities, we're tempted to think that security lies back there somewhere, and we somehow feel better thinking about the security of the past. Despite the attractiveness of this illusion, we need to recognize it as illusion, nothing more, albeit an illusion with power to keep us from conceding that some realities are now gone forever.

There are some memories we cling to, and others we wish nothing more than just to jettison once and for all. It is natural that we wish to separate happy from painful ones, but one thing we cannot do—we cannot underestimate the strength of cither positive or negative memories and their power to claim our thoughts when there is little else in our lives that can occupy us so powerfully.

Curiously, nearly everyone gets caught up in this backward pull, even when we recognize in advance how painful and counter-productive it will prove to be. It tends to bring life to a halt, but we still are drawn to the past and wish that we might experience it all once more. We don't want to let go of what was dear and meaningful. Though we treasure memories of the past, we must be honest about the reality behind those memories and allow an upholding God to assuage the pain that is part of letting go. Otherwise we suffer needlessly.

You'll find that the more the future seems denied you, the more the past reasserts itself. But to settle for this as an unchangeable status is to drop anchor in an unsafe haven, refusing to move and abandoning the main currents of life for a placid dead end.

Is this not little more than the past reintroducing itself as compensation for the vision of a diminished future?

Eyes on the Future

When one is no longer active enough to participate in history making, he must then resign himself either to experiencing the history being made without him, or as someone said, he must write about it. How many retired professionals chafe for an opportunity to once again contribute in some way to the making of history? Not finding that opportunity, they review the past for reaffirmation that they once were history makers. This cannot be taken away from them.

Clearly, then, the challenge is a dedicated discipline of letting go, refusing to turn back, accepting the fact that former times cannot be lived again and people and places lost to us cannot be brought back. We must find peace in the hope that associations will be renewed in the future life promised to all believers. Strong resolve is required to turn away from the past and take a firm grasp on the present, fixing our eyes on the future just ahead. If we cannot quite do this on our own, then we should find a person or group who can support us in this process.

Jack Hayford offers some sound counsel: "May we learn to live in that quiet, 'waiting' mode which the Holy Spirit works in those who choose to wait on God to secure our tomorrows, rather than pressuring to 'fix' them ourselves."[5] C. S. Lewis was correct when he commented: "There are better things ahead than any we leave behind." We must believe this even before we see it become reality.

So don't let the past blind-side you! Rather, let the living God empower your new steps through his planned present and his promising future!

> Not for one single day
> Can I discern the way,
> But this I surely know:
> Who gives the day
> Will show the way,
> So I securely go.
>
> John Oxenham[6]

6

Moving beyond Yesterday

W hat's ahead for me now? That's the question that plagues all men as they move into retirement. For most retirees it is tempting to long for a past that is now gone and frightening to look ahead to an uncertain future. Expectations for the future, or more precisely the lack thereof, make this transition a disabling one if not a downright traumatic one. The question of how to move beyond yesterday is the tough issue at the psychological heart of retirement.

Understandably, because the future is unknown, there may be over-expectations, false expectations, or expectations never thoroughly thought through. For a variety of reasons, retiring may not turn out to be what it was thought to be—often it will be less, sometimes far less. This becomes serious when a retiree can't help sizing up the present and feeling he isn't worth much anymore if his tomorrows are not making good on promises he thought they'd made and if he can't trade in his yesterdays for a fulfilling future. We're not talking about retirement blues—something most of us could handle. This is called reactive depression and is far more debilitating.

Well into my own retirement, loss of the sense of self-worth came on the heels of a generally hopeless outlook. Temporarily, life became like a tunnel I couldn't see through. With recovery came the renewed desire to move beyond yesterday and grasp the present life of promise.

Work Ethic or Worth Ethic?

Lee Butcher touches on this in his book *Retirement without Fear*.[1] He cites a University of Michigan study of America's work ethic and concludes that along with having a work ethic we need a comparable "worth" ethic. What this involves, fundamentally, is recognizing that worth derives from who we are, not from what we do. It is the person, not just the work, that has value.

To illustrate, my former professions as pastor, professor, counselor, and writer did not define me as a person, special to God and to his kingdom. Whatever worth the work itself may have had it was not the basis for calculating my personal worth.

The key is to see ourselves as one designed by God the way he wants us to be. Ultimately, what we are to him is what gives us value, causing true worth to reside in us. It can never be the worth of what we do or have done, not even what we do or have done for God and his Kingdom. Each of us must see beyond the achievement self-concept we've contrived for ourselves. As a unique, valued person, each of us is meant to reflect God's design for his redeemed ones. Created in his image, we come from individual molds and are meant for individual ends.

To remove wrong-headed views of personal worth based on work, the retiree needs what Paul Tournier calls "reconversion"—restored ability to see personal life as a developing whole; that is, one's personhood continues to advance right on through the stages of one's entire life span. Reconversion enables the retiree to respond to new meanings that are a part of each major transition. New interests, new activities, new relationships must find their places in his life if his retirement years are to be meaningful. This personal growth can counter the negative effects of having left a long-time career.

Each of us is responsible for not allowing himself to retire into apathy and passivity. We're tempted in this direction until we learn how to handle the replacement of former life patterns with new ones. If our gaze is fixed on what we've left behind, how can we hope to discover new meanings, new interests, and new objectives awaiting us? This tendency to live in the past is eliminated once we recognize that our worth does not reside in reclaiming, repeating, or achieving in the same way the things we did in the past.

The Best of the Past and the Present

Retirees soon find how diversely populated is the world they now inhabit. If they've relocated, the problem is enhanced. They must establish a whole new circle of relationships. Even a new church fellowship contributes to this difficult readjustment.

Inwardly, it's easy to pout: "New friends aren't like the old ones." They aren't, but they can become good friends just the same. We've found this with our friends, Torval and Hilja. There could not be a closer, more meaningful bond. Truth is, deep friendships can be long-term or very recent. Length of time does not determine their depth.

If in your retirement you have the added stress of being in a new location, then new friendships need to be developed as quickly as possible. It may have been a while since you realized that making new friends is not easy, especially when you've been so secure with the old ones. Still, new friendships are attainable if you expend the necessary effort. This can be a delightful and profitable way to use your newly gained leisure. As friends and favorite places of your then and there are replaced by friends and places of your here and now, they help you recover normal life patterns.

In retirement we do not lose entirely the essential continuity of former life patterns; many routines remain very much intact. Our personal world doesn't change altogether; there is much that we bring with us. We're not orphaned from our past, although at first it may seem so when some things must be relinquished. It's doubtful that many of us stopped long enough to ask, "What are the over-arching purposes to which I've committed myself that still remain intact and can reach meaningfully into the future? Which ones will not? How will my personal relationships change or remain the same? What about my relationship to the Lord and service for him?" It all just seems to happen, but because of the abiding continuity, all necessary changes are manageable.

In my retirement what I needed to learn was that the quality of successful retirement lies in moving as quickly as possible from concentrating on what is being given up to holding as valuable that which is being taken up. The key here is quick and positive replacement.

Coming to Terms with Leisure

During our career years, we often felt we were up to our eyeballs in work. The thought of having leisure time hardly entered our minds, and we certainly didn't plan for what we would do with it in retirement other than looking forward to time for hobbies and travel.

In order to adequately think through the full meaning of our personal existence as retired Christians, we have to fully consider the place of this newfound luxury called leisure. It's strange that the very leisure we looked forward to now becomes a potential problem—even a burden.

During working years, leisure consisted of brief,

intermittent breaks extracted from busy work schedules. Generally, family activities were planned for set times, usually coming during the summer when the children were out of school. There were also a few long-weekend holidays or days taken off from time to time for leisure purposes or "sick days." These were brief respites sandwiched into an otherwise unrelieved occupational grind.

During midlife years, when the nest emptied, leisure scheduling became more opportune, more flexible. For the first time there was a taste of what leisure could offer a couple freed from other obligations—doubtless, a preview of retirement. But was it exactly?

Now, in retirement, a radical exchange takes place. Short, intermittent leisure times are exchanged for an entirely new life of long-term leisure. This leisure time commands our attention and planning as serious business. It's now at the forefront of everything because it occupies such a large portion of our lives.

With a whole new stage of life characterized by leisure, the question arises, What do I do with unlimited time for myself? Will it be employed for trivial ends or for worthy ends that satisfy my inner person and truly lead to personal growth? There is a whole new freedom to choose either the trivial or the worthy.

This is important, for daily patterns from now on will be organized around this new leisure mode, and soon enough these patterns will come to characterize the whole final stretch of active years.

Have you thought how little resemblance there is between your former leisure and retirement's long-term, open-ended leisure? They are altogether different in two fundamental respects—structure and meaning. Leisure is no longer structured around brief intermittent periods and set times, sandwiched where possible. Nor is its meaning essentially recreational. The new leisure mode has the potential for all kinds of positive things, but what are potentially hazardous are the unforeseen and unexpected reactions to it.

Negative reactions can range from simple disappointment and frustration to regression into self. For some, gripping anxieties are triggered (not fatal but crippling), for others, hopelessness of their prospects for both a stable present and future (near fatal!).

Unfortunately, adjustment to the new leisure doesn't come naturally or automatically. If it is entered unrealistically or without a definite plan, the potential for disorientation, depression, even dysfunction is very real. Not a pleasant outlook! I'm still aware of the wounds of a leisure lifestyle for which I had not made adequate plans.

Balancing Leisure with Meaningful Self-Occupation

It remains a curious thing why—if having chafed because our work years didn't provide enough leisure—now in retirement we chafe because unlimited leisure confuses us and isn't found sufficiently challenging. Where is the balance between living with leisure and meaningful work or self-occupation?

Does talk about balancing leisure and work strike

you as incongruous since retirees are forever through with work? Isn't that what retirement's all about?

Well, no. Work is not exchanged for leisure. Both continue on, but in new proportions and suited to new life-objectives. And let's be quick to say that both are needed, but in retirement a new balance must be struck between leisure and a worthy self-occupation.

We can understand Paul Tournier's insistence that work and leisure are both necessary and complementary to each other. Both are meant to contribute to the development of whole people. "Work brings development in depth because of the specialization it requires. Leisure counterbalances it with development in breadth because of the diversity of interests it cultivates."[2]

One misleading notion is that leisure is the reward for work well done. On every hand we see evidence of leisure being made the goal toward which working years are directed. While ours is a culture that values work in its own right as well as for its material and personal rewards, almost at the same height is the elevation of leisure as life's chief reward. Someone has said that we Americans take work leisurely and work hard at our leisure!

With the advent of retirement, leisure is expected to be maximized. So the theme is constantly drummed into us: "Retire as early as possible; enjoy the American dream!" Fortunately, in recent years there has been much rethinking on the advantages and disadvantages of early retirement. Man does not live by leisure alone! Many men find themselves retiring from retirement!

This whole notion of leisure as reward puts work and leisure in false juxtaposition, the result being that both are denigrated. Properly seen, each exists for its own sake, and each is meant to continue in a healthy symbiotic relationship with the other.

If work was once an idol, care must be taken not to now substitute leisure as the new idol, to value leisure as an end in itself. Like all idols, it will turn to emptiness. Viewed correctly we look at leisure as providing conditions that make possible, first, a range of occupational options—full- or part-time, voluntary or compensated, along familiar lines of work or entirely new—and second, opportunities for growth as a person. What leisure affords, first and foremost, is greater freedom of choice, enabling us to be and do as we desire, as we think best.

My mistake was that I concentrated first and foremost on the question of what would occupy me in a productive sense. Little did I consider how I might take advantage of the opportunity leisure afforded to simply develop as a whole person and let my life be one of service. This faulty emphasis proved a great part of my ensuing problems.

Contrary to expectation, assimilation to the new leisure doesn't come naturally or automatically to many people. Any number of things—many psychological—can impede progress toward a satisfactory adjustment to leisure. Studies at the University of California at Berkeley found, for example, that

many retirees mourn their loss of regular employment as if grieving the death of a loved one. Leisure
has not satisfied their deep need to be meaningfully
occupied.

As far back as 1929 Sigmund Freud noted in *Civi-
lization and Its Discontents*: "Work binds the individual more closely to reality [and] the human community."[3] How true this is in our time. There's an
unmistakable bond between work and the reality of
human community as we experience it. It is natural,
then, that men are drawn to want some continuing
work experience to balance whatever leisure pursuits
they choose.

Develop a Strategy

In retirement, with a desire for both leisure and
work, men must think through how to take circumstances in hand and proceed to make those circumstances work for them—an active rather than passive
response. Even in retirement, they still need to take
charge.

If in this process we find that we are somewhat
adrift on an uncertain sea, we should not blame circumstances. Inertia, apathy, or lack of imagination,
effort, or will, one of these may turn out to be the
cause. To make our new situation what we want it to
be, we first need to adopt a thought-out strategy for
finding a satisfactory combination of leisure and a
gratifying sense of productivity. There's little use waiting for a winning strategy to come to us; we must
reach out, find it, seize it.

If you're anything like I am, perhaps you assume things will generally take care of themselves without too much concern and with a minimum of planning. For example, I assumed that writing would suffice as my major occupation in retirement and so gave little thought to other possibilities. I had little concern for matters such as community involvement or social relationships. And I thought little about using my retirement years for personal development. My vision, as I see it now, was extremely short-sighted.

Looking back, I wonder how much any one of us did during career years to determine what would be the overall meaning of our ongoing years, meaning significant enough to cover a life span? Did our planning (if we did any) include both leisure and occupational choices for the final years? Did we see the need back then? In other words, did we do our thinking in advance, or merely idealistically contemplate an idyllic life no longer driven by pressures and responsibilities? All along did we foresee that retirement would have special demands—declining health, for example? Or did we just suppose that everything would somehow take care of itself, whether planned for or not? Was our planning limited to such things as finances and where we'd live? Did we find it difficult to concentrate on career and at the same time reflect seriously on things so distant as retirement? More critically, did we simply let present demands effectively blank out all thought of future readjustments? There are things the soon-to-be-retired need to think about.

Along with a well-thought-out strategy for retirement years, there should be a backup plan in case circumstances at retirement time are different from those you envisioned. I had no backup plan and certainly no thought for utilizing the years ahead chiefly for personal development.

Gerontologists agree that people who never learned along the way to look for the fundamental meaning of their lives are unlikely to organize their thoughts sufficiently when retired to find that meaning—at least quickly or without help.

Multitudes of retirees could repeat Montaigne's insight: "To retire successfully is no easy matter." For any of us to determine beforehand what's most important down the line—for instance, to what values we'll devote our final years—is no easy matter. Yet failure to anticipate and plan in the past does not mean that it can't be started now. Those who look to God for guidance, who give solid thought as well as prayer to what their lives can be develop a successful strategy. Planning, whether we like it or not, is a form of necessary work.

Developing Maturity of the Person

Viennese psychologist Carl Jung speaks of two turning points in every adult life. The first one comes when we move from the youthful years of preparation into the period covered by working years. During this stage, we learn to embrace a dual existence—the combining of career and family life. This is when family development is crucial and career demands uppermost. Economic well-being and professional status pretty generally win out. So often these turn out to be the years when the spouse at home has the full brunt of raising the family and organizing family life.

The second turning point, Jung suggests, takes a man from career into what he calls "culture." "Culture" for Jung is the final period of one's life span when the focus turns to completing the process of personal maturing. No longer does the dual existence of career and family vie for first place—with career winning! Family life is now established, children are raised and gone, career goals by and large have been met, and now new horizons loom ahead. For Jung this is when one is beyond career and free to develop individual personhood with all the exciting possibilities of an expanded personal life. Jung believes this process follows an unquestioned law that human life is meant to move forward until no longer possible. Pragmatically, what personal life becomes at this time is what each one individually makes it.

For a person not to advance toward more complete human fulfillment at this stage, says Jung, is failure to see that when we refuse to grow old we are like children who refuse to leave their childhood. Now is the time for reawakening and completing everything that so long has been sacrificed to career ends.

Under the pressures of career demands, the working individual never truly breaks free to mature as a person, not until retirement forces freedom upon him. Then at last he has the chance to be, as Jung puts it, "an original," discovering "the values of personality."

The development of this theme can be found in Jung's book *Psychology of the Spirit*. With a new beginning a person can develop what is so altogether important—a unique, mature, self-fulfilled human personhood. Additionally, the Christian man has the opportunity to become a person mature in the life Christ gives, to truly be Christ's man, infused with the nature of Christ, allowing his personality to be increasingly conformed to Christ's likeness. A committed person is able to concentrate on the Kingdom of God ("Seek first the Kingdom of God and his righteousness"). At long last, personal life can be devoted to the high goal of becoming what God wants each child of his to be.

Through what means is this maturity possible? For starters—through extended times of meditation on Scripture and through obedience to the inner urgings of the Spirit. Included, too, would be becoming an "unbound" ambassador to the world's needs. As never before, one is free to seek the mind of Christ for ways to serve the cause of the gospel at home and, who knows, perhaps in other parts of the world. No longer do career obligations stand in the way of advancing in these new and wider directions. For many retirees today, neither economic nor health factors will stand in the way.

In our working years, routine work demands invariably obscured serious voids in personal life. Even when we did recognize those voids, we tended to plunge relentlessly into our work, attempting to blunt the recognition and the urge to make a needed course correction. But just because we submerged the awareness of these voids doesn't mean that they went away, and now that time is our own, in all likelihood these voids will become even more prominent and will demand that they be worked on in earnest.

Because retirement forces us to measure personal success in altogether different terms than we are used to, it is incumbent on us to negotiate the Jungian second turning point, to advance toward completing "maturity of the person." At center stage from here on is the matter of completing our growth as a person. Psychologists, following Jung's lead, call this "interiorization"—finding the qualities each of us has within himself or herself, latent qualities perhaps not previously recognized.

What I am seeking to emphasize is this. No longer are we retirees still in the years of greatest deployment of talent and energy, our peak years of attainment. Back then we lived by and for the "externals"—our career accomplishments—which symbolized success. Now it is the "internals"—the interior life—that should receive our attention. In the development of mature personhood with its own unique possibilities, externals take an ever-diminishing place, and rightfully so.

This point is not lost on contemporary psychologists. Roger L. Gould, in his early book *Transformations: Growth and Change in Adult Life*, concurs: "Our sense of meaning resides within us; it does not inhere in any extension of us that can be amputated by the wheel of fortune."[4]

Thus, the value we place on self is no longer to be based on things outside self but inside self. We must learn to lead our lives, based on those values, and not to be led. We are to organize our own lives ourselves rather than live them as they were organized for us by career forces.

The option is now ours: Either we decide our own future objectives or by default lose out. If we don't decide on our objectives by ourselves, they will once again be dictated by forces outside ourselves—objectives we wouldn't have chosen for ourselves. We must never again be in bondage to externals. For a retiree who is alive in spirit, such a course would prove intolerable and would be self-defeating, for the retiree is at last fully in control of his own life. His own ideals, values, and personal objectives can now replace former career aims.

Moreover, if later years are to be meaningful at all, one cannot merely devote energies to diversions that have no essential or lasting value. Even a strong focus on hobbies suggests that life has turned in on itself, has given itself over to things that cannot truly nurture the human spirit.

Speaking personally, it was when my hobbies of boating and fishing proved less than satisfying that I came to a clearer recognition that an adequate life for me, now that I was freed from obligatory work, would not afford contentment when filled merely with hobbies, sports, and entertaining diversions. The very word *diversion* suggests something that is non-essential. There's a sinister implication in the term *diversion* (a life course diverted?).

Beyond question, hobbies make for a healthy and welcome change—when diversionary change is what we need at a given time. They are attractive alternatives meant to break up the sameness of work, to reinvigorate body and spirit. The "re-creating" of physical and spiritual vitality is the true intent of all recreation and a positive thing. But when recreation or hobbies are all that fill up and give meaning to our lives, how swiftly they lose their worth!

We need to recognize that the process of finding a proper balance may be arduous, that today's popular cultural values tend to be deceptively attractive, that often more satisfying values are less compelling because less well-known. And, strangely, never at the start do we seem aware of the long-term effects leisure choices will have on us, especially choices of only transient value. We become what we choose!

Trying to adjust the past to the present, one of the first things I did, three years into our retirement, was to take old class lectures and research files used in the sociology of marriage course, many years' collections of articles, even a great many sermons and biblical files, and to discard it all. How's that for closure with a vengeance! I slammed the door on my professional past. Family and friends were aghast! Whether I was being wise or simply reactionary, I'm not sure. But it was closure.

Not that I regretted saying good-bye to those artifacts of a career now behind me. Problem was, I had not at that point replaced my professional attachments with anything appropriate to my new life. By discarding so much of my past, I had merely moved into a personal vacuum.

As I began to feel the discomfort of the vacuum that I had created I, like many others, unwittingly fell back into thinking that it was my occupation that had given worth and meaning to my life. But let's face it, that basis was now gone. I had placed two realities—value of work on one hand and meaning of life on the other—in wrong juxtaposition. They were incorrectly reversed. It is the individual himself who gives worth and meaning to work—not the other way around. Having achieved recognition and status through an occupation, having also enjoyed the self-esteem and reward that goes with it, these are not tantamount to having reached personal maturity, or to having fulfilled some highly valued human end. In fact, inner growth may well be impeded by career success and the false meaning such success gives to personal worth.

It is always a mistake to give primacy to "doing" over "being." What we do is bound to change as life's circumstances change and the very thing we relied on to give status and meaning to our lives is then removed. This is exactly what happens in retirement. If during our working years it was work that dignified self, most likely after our work has been laid down we'll continue to let whatever we choose to do dignify self rather than, properly, let self dignify our occupational choice.

Developing New Relationships

Paul Tournier makes a significant point: Professional success depends on competence in one's field. So quite naturally, specialized conversations form the bond between people who work together. There is commonality in working at and talking about the same thing. But in the process of developing that specialized mode of conversation, we tend to leave undeveloped the speech and actions of personal relationships. Come retirement, we no longer relate through specialized conversations and functions. From then on those former bonding agents cease to exist.

Once we're retired and outside vocational circles, we soon find we have little to talk about that fits the general population of retirees. People don't want to hear long discourses on what we've done, who we've known, where we've been. The danger is in becoming ingrown—talking largely to ourselves. So here we are, beginners again, learning that falling back on our specialized talk doesn't suffice to build new relationships. But we can't satisfactorily engage others with merely superficial conversation. We have to work at broadening our base of interests, which in turn broadens the content of our conversation. At the same time we must listen with a new pair of ears!

It is, you see, a matter of altering our conversations to a more personal mode to fit a more personal pattern of living, gradually moving away from former interests and on to new ones. Since we can only talk about what we know, we must expand our perspectives and enter a larger world.

Another problem Tournier observes is that in our working years closely bonded relationships were built in with the job. The bonding agent in the workplace was talk and action that was most conducive to getting the job done. The end in view was reaching organizational targets. Relationships were, as the sociologists say, "formal," aimed at smooth functioning in the organization. We related, abstractly speaking, as "functionaries" (and what could be less personal than a "functionary"!).

When I left Westmont College and my colleagues there, it did not occur to me that since in retirement circles I would no longer be talking only with sociologists, faculty members, college personnel, nor pastors that the nature of my conversations would change radically. Certain elements would be dropped out and new ones added. My new world included retired businessmen, clerks, farmers, construction workers—men of all backgrounds.

We found, however, that if we kept up with the local, national, and international current affairs, we had much in common to talk about. In the church we could share interests in the things of Christ, and thus find a common language. Around our mutual faith and concern for the church's ministry in the world, our roles were brought closer. Developing and nurturing relationships such as these take time and a commitment to keep at it through the uncomfortable beginning stages until strong bonds are formed.

When we were working we had little time to commit to friendships. We may spend eight hours a day side by side with people at work, yet off the job have little to show socially for those relationships. Usually we find it's better not to know our colleagues intimately, for when we do we may allow personal concerns and emotions to intrude on the efficiency of our tasks. Little did most of us recognize that work roles actually limited any well-rounded social development, and the training we received on the job did not prepare us for genuine personal interaction.

Professionals learn to distance themselves from those both higher and lower on the echelon, to maintain social distance for the sake of their work relationships. It's true that, on occasion, close relationships in the workplace tend to develop in questionable ways. But if only we had eyes to see the personal deprivation of purely formal relationships!

Sadly, this formal mode of relating demands a price—a certain inner distancing from co-workers. They can know us professionally but not personally, and it is our loss that we learn to keep them at arm's length. We pass through our careers as underdeveloped individuals because we have not learned how to have intimate, trusting relationships.

In retirement, the network of personal relationships undergoes a radical change; retirees must learn to relate on altogether different terms if they're to relate successfully at all. Social interaction is less formal, more personal, not structured according to a hierarchy based on status or prominence. (Ever notice that retirees are the "huggiest" of people!)

For the most part, retirees naturally hunger for more personal, less official relationships—the very thing they've been deprived of. And whether consciously or not, they are to some extent making up for relationships left behind. But most importantly, they are seeking social linkage, which has been undeveloped during the work years. Most succeed in establishing this social linkage while others refuse to give it the effort necessary. A few who crave friendships pursue this course too aggressively because they want them immediately. For most retirees, this is a gradual learning process.

Establishing new relationships late in life can be a difficult task. Some retirees think of themselves as failures if they do not find their place in their new environment as quickly as hoped. They tend to give up too soon. Sadly, their focus is on what appears to them as their own inability to make new friends. People they meet seem different from those they left behind (really, only different because not familiar). The complaint is widespread yet perfectly easy to understand.

Developing Positive Uses of Time

For those who think themselves failures, in whatever aspect of retirement, it's tempting to retreat inside themselves, to settle for an unnecessarily restricted lifestyle. To them, the very word "retire" sounds similar to "retreat," and to retreat is exactly what people do who think themselves failures. Do you see yourself retreating? Have you settled for the false image named failure?

It becomes easy for people to brood about the past when they feel lost in a new setting. They rehash the past and use subtle mind games to indulge negative reminiscences. Some repeatedly call up seeming injustices they experienced—someone who blocked their vocational progress or an individual with less ability who connived, and took, the promotion he had not earned.

With little else to think about, people can spend inordinate amounts of time brooding about these things, but negative thinking only retards a person's assimilation to a successful retirement lifestyle. Negative thinking must be recognized for what it is and renounced, something that may take a gigantic effort.

Hopefully, discouraged and defeated retirees will meet others who've triumphed over the same initial difficulties. With this help from the sidelines, they themselves can move on to higher ground, to more positive expectations. Victory is never far removed from defeat.

Have you met the retiree who blithely states he's "just happily occupying time"? Or worse still, "killing time"?

Time is used in many different ways by different people. It can be used productively or it can be wasted, used unwisely, but never "killed." The very notion of "killing time" not only obscures the possibility of finding a satisfying self-occupation but totally negates the vision of advancing in personal maturity.

Is this not a mind-set symptomatic of aimlessness? When one has lost sight of life's meaning? The great need of the retiree is to find meaningful employment of mind and resources that will ensure a full future. For many, this means a "second career," perhaps part-time, perhaps nonremunerative, but nonetheless a career—what we shall refer to as a "free career"—non-obligatory, freely chosen, where the individual sets the parameters to fit his new status and to meet his own personal needs and wishes. This concept will be explored in the next chapter.

> And whatever work you may have to do, do every-thing in the name of the Lord Jesus, thanking God the Father through him.
>
> [Colossians 3:17 *Phillips*]

7

New Life Parameters

In the previous chapter it was suggested that what retirees need more than mere diversions or hobbies is meaningful self-occupation. A second career can meet the need for self-occupation. This should not be confused with another full-time paid vocation. It is not merely exchanging one workplace for another or one obligatory job for another. Self-occupation is work that provides something personally satisfying, something that fulfills a socially worthwhile end. The criteria is this: A chosen occupation must meet the individual's need to occupy time in a worthy manner, devote thought and energy to some good project, and at the same time not feel under obligation or stress.

Concept of the Free Career

With a tinge of facetiousness, Simone de Beauvoir saw retirement as relatively easy going for one segment of retirees. She observed that people who have already chosen mediocrity will not have much difficulty in fitting themselves in, and trimming their lives. What is her point? Retirement ought to elevate the thoughtful among us above mediocrity and to challenge our striving toward the highest ends. It is especially true for those whose careers were not mediocre—they will be unsatisfied if they allow their retirement self-occupation to be mediocre.

My own problem with retirement came at this point: How can I live out my life and make a contribution that elevates the daily routine above mere mediocrity? What worthy and gratifying enterprise is there to choose that will occupy this final stretch of less-encumbered years?

Surely, of all people, Christians ought not to be satisfied with offering the Lord mediocrity, whether in lifework or in retirement pursuits! What takes on ultimate importance, then, is the quality of truly self-giving Christian service. A "free career" in retirement can meet the need to make a valued contribution.

A free career is a specific occupation, chosen not out of necessity but solely because it is interesting and has objectives considered worthy of fullhearted participation. It is not a mere time-filling diversion; neither is it time-restrictive as is a full-time career that is pursued to meet economic needs and professional goals.

Fundamentally, free careers are governed by a distinct motivation that rises above self-aggrandizement or even self-fulfillment. At the very heart of such an occupation is some intrinsic social benefit that beckons one's enthusiastic participation and makes life count for good. In the free career, working relationships are structured along the lines of social interaction, unlike former working relationships that served to promote corporate goals. This makes free careers truly appropriate for retired people.

Commitment to a free career ought to be validated through some quantifiable measures, but not those of our working years. Now we can seek growth in maturity, development of satisfying relationships, use of personal gifts, and some social good resulting from our work. Remember, it's not the work that validates the worker; the worker validates the work!

About free careers Paul Tournier asserts: "This reconversion from the first to the second career implies an inner conversion. If there remains a secret nostalgia for the old working life, its joys and even its sorrows, its struggles and its victories, the social status it conferred, and the exciting feeling of being part of a large-scale enterprise, of engaging in an industrial or scientific adventure—that secret nostalgia is a great obstacle to the birth of a valid second career. Imprisoned by his past, the retired person is not free enough in his mind to construct a new future."[1]

Equally pertinent is Tournier's word: "If one dwells on one's past working life, either regretting it or complaining about it, going back to it in thought and spirit when one can no longer return to it in reality, one drains the present of its colour, and deprives oneself of the joys that may be found in a second career."[2]

We're not talking, you see, about an economic undertaking as such. Nor is this a trivial pursuit— merely a nice way to keep busy. Rather, it is a response to an inner call for a quality existence—the personally meaningful use of time, thought, energy, and resources. A free career makes it possible to pursue the two goals of maturing as a person and reaching out to help others.

What one chooses to do should be, as far as possible, free from stress. Nothing in a free career should wear unduly on one's physical or emotional health. It should also be relatively free from drudgery. Not that every aspect of the task shall be stimulating, even fulfilling, but the goal of a free career is, first, development of the inner person, then second, engagement in something that has intrinsic worth—valued simply in the doing. Of course, there should also be sufficient opportunities for accomplishment to buoy up your spirit and motivate endurance so that you won't be bored. Where the task is right and the ends worthy, then inner satisfaction will transcend any transient drudgery or uninspired moments.

The partial ministry I assumed as a volunteer at the San Jose church I had loved and left thirty years before worked well. I had no problem working under another pastor. So it was right at the time, for about a year, a very blessed year! Then I had to realize that the task-related stresses were greater than I wanted to handle. This was not a problem with authority but with the demands on time and energy.

A special aspect of free careers is the place of spontaneity and imagination. Free careers are governed more by what is creative and socially meaningful than by impersonal contacts of the kind found in the business and professional world. It is for these reasons that new self-occupations are freeing to the participants.

This is not to say free careers cannot be financially profitable ventures; not at all. My retirement occupation, for example, is writing—serving the Lord through the printed page. The income from my writing is not great but most welcome. But, you see, compensation is neither the primary motivation nor the ultimate satisfaction. The point of a free career is that the compelling necessity is not earnings but personal gratification. The more important objective is the making of a contribution to people's lives in the name of the Savior. If there is remuneration, that's an added benefit. Of course, where additional income is needed to provide a quality retirement, that must factor in.

Choosing a Free Career

Retirement careers are often a matter of giving something a try, finding out if it's right, then either settling into the role or moving to something else. There aren't the same high stakes as with a first career, and a person needn't make the same investment of self to succeed. No corporate ladder beckons; there is no association of professionals competing and evaluating one another; and no one is trying to make a personal statement about his expertise. His challenge is simply to give the new role a try and find what is best for him.

Many in retirement will have the same struggles I did. I had the notion that in retirement I still had a statement to make and had to find roles that were compatible with my professional past. I wanted to see myself, and have others see me, as a professional. But this only precluded numerous avenues of useful service and self-fulfillment.

There's no reason not to pursue many possibilities for a free career and through the retirement years to undertake several different ones. Time isn't pressing; a choice needn't be made quickly. Nothing this time around need threaten either present or future welfare. Surprisingly, endeavors we once thought uninviting may turn out to be highly interesting when we give them a try. So often what creates and sustains the new interest is association with a new group of people—probably different from those with whom we had former ties, yet well worth knowing. It takes time to feel comfortable with people we've known for only a short while, so we must nurture those new contacts and give the process time. The new circle may become our close friends.

What I'm commending is willingness to explore a broad range of possibilities, ruling out none at first, then taking the plunge and taking time to see if it was a good choice.

Dealing with Authority

For a great number of professional and business retirees, the most difficult adjustment comes when they're no longer the people in charge, no longer the ones who occupy the top rung on the ladder, no longer wielding authority. Many men find that the adjustment can be made rather easily, but for others it's best and perfectly all right to avoid any retirement occupation where the question of authority would be problematic. This is not an uncommon problem on church boards when retired pastors are asked to serve. The retired pastor may find it difficult to be a member of a board that has had less experience than he has. Likewise, church boards or volunteer groups are sometimes uncomfortable with retirees who bring a recognized background of professional competence— and who have a need to exercise it. This might also be the case for a retiree who is under a manager less capable than himself or for a retiree who has recently relinquished a position of authority and in his free career is supervised by a younger person. Subordination to a younger person has different ramifications for different individuals, but if it's a problem, it should be avoided. The retiree who finds himself in such a situation should leave it for something else. He's not a quitter, just wise enough to know when something doesn't work. Remember, the fundamental expectation of the free career is that it be attractive, continually inviting, free from stress or conflict, and personally fulfilling. Submitting to certain forms of authority may mean forfeiting some of the benefits of your retirement career.

Competence Isn't Everything

Whatever work one enters in a free career, there is an inclination to think that one must sustain the same highly trained, broadly experienced expertise that was developed and essential in the first career. How deeply ingrained in business and professional culture is the principle that competence is everything!—as it should be. This assumption only places unwelcome pressure on the individual who has looked forward to busyness with joy, not stress. In the free career, which is by nature noncompetitive, the retiree does not have to maintain that same level of competence. This is what can make the free career enjoyable.

Don't Be Impatient

Along with a natural anxiety in facing an uncertain future, or trying out what may not be the final retirement occupation, there is the tendency of long-term "doers" from business or the professions to succumb rather readily to impatience. Being used to seeing things done promptly and assuredly, the task of searching and experimenting, of having to try what may prove not to be appropriate may try one's patience.

Whenever I tend to become impatient I recall the moving story told by Zorba the Greek, in the novel by Kazantzakis.

> I remember one morning when I discovered a cocoon in the bark of a tree, just as the butterfly was making a hole in its case and preparing to come out. I waited

awhile, but it was too long appearing and I was impatient. I bent over it and breathed on it to warm it. I warmed it as quickly as I could and the miracle began to happen before my eyes, faster than life. The case opened, the butterfly started slowly crawling out and I shall never forget my horror when I saw how its wings were folded back and crumpled; the wretched butterfly tried with its whole trembling body to unfold them. Bending over it, I tried to help it with my breath. In vain. It needed to be hatched out patiently, and the unfolding of the wings should be a gradual process in the sun. Now, it was too late. My breath had forced the butterfly to appear all crumpled before its time. It struggled desperately and, a few seconds later, died in the palm of my hand.[3]

Our temptation is to help God unfold his plan by intruding with our own helpfulness, but the sad consequence often is that we destroy the very opportunity God wants to place before us. I like Kazantzakis's thoughtful conclusion: "We should not hurry, we should not be impatient, but we should confidently obey the eternal rhythm."

God knows our need as we make the enormous adjustments of retirement, and he has a plan for the fulfillment of our life. We must learn to wait on him and not impatiently flail around on our own. He will direct us to the place or places he wants us to be.

Don't Be Fearful

Together with the uncertainty of finding our place and the impatience of getting things settled and life on track once more, there may be the fear of not suc-

ceeding. Retirees who have completed very successful careers may be particularly anxious to look good
in the eyes of others. A man soon forgets what it was
like in earlier days, when he had to prove himself,
work his way up, gain self-confidence and the acceptance of others. Now, he's starting again, and even
though it's his free career, old concerns about quali-
fying and being accepted return. It's understandable
that there is resistance to moving out and moving on.

Inertia is also a problem that keeps retirees from
moving out and moving on. The longer one waits to
move ahead, the greater the inertia.

Accept the Encouragement of Others

Concerns like these may suggest confiding in
another retiree whose background is similar and who
has already made the grade in a free career. It may
have been difficult because of professional pride and
autonomy in the past to lean on others, but now it is
wise to do so. How reassuring to see others who've
gained new enthusiasm, who are fitting into previously unfamiliar spheres, making new friends, doing
totally new things—and loving their new life!

Being together with successful retirees, one soon
discovers how typical it is, first, to explore various
avenues, to tentatively move ahead, make mistakes,
try second and third times, then have a few laughs
about misadventures along the way. Finally the right
course does appear; yes, there was a solution out there
waiting!

Professionals are not accustomed to laughing about
their own mistakes in front of peers. They have a hard

time acknowledging even small mistakes. The joy of a free career is that you needn't fear admitting mistakes. It's comfortable to know you can afford to laugh at yourself. There's an easygoing camaraderie in exploring occupational possibilities, sharing common anxiety about starting out in new directions, even having to say, "This isn't it."

When a retiree finds the place where he should be and settles in, he feels reinstated in the flow of life. Self-confidence quickly returns. Forging new social linkage is stimulating. Successfully undertaking something never tried before is enriching and rewarding. Inevitably, too, the right free career has the reward of taking a person further than first expected. It's a stretching experience—one guaranteed to bring both genuine growth and usefulness.

8

Learning to Live with the Unfinished

When retirees fail to grow and experience a solid sense of life's ultimate meaning, there may develop both physical and emotional dysfunction. Viktor Frankl of Vienna, father of logotherapy, finds that modern man's "existential void" is a cause of neuroses. In the retirement crisis Frankl sees an "unemployment neurosis." Others besides Frankl have found that such ill effects as diseases and physical degeneration result from the malaise of retirement. It is well established that life and health are closely bound up with (1) a sense of personal fulfillment and (2) whether or not life continues to be meaningful.

Perhaps this helps explain the alarming fact that twice the number of men as women over sixty-five commit suicide. These are not all for the same reason, but health problems rank highest. Just the physical limitations that develop during retirement cause people to look back to times when they could do so much more of what they wanted to do. Sometimes unemployment neuroses—purposelessness and inability to cope—bring a swifter decline in health, and together these lead to a person's putting an end to it all.

Paul Tournier says that not one of us ever comes to the place where career success or development of personhood can assure complete human fulfillment. Realistically, we ought not expect it. In a splendid chapter on acceptance, Tournier says, "The particular acceptance I am referring to here is perhaps one of the most difficult to achieve; it is acceptance of unfulfillment. That is one of the great problems of retirement. . . . Professional life is over, and it finishes unfinished."[1] Thus our task is to learn to take in stride this "acceptance of the unfulfilled," knowing there are ways to deal with it in positive terms.

To be sure, there are those of us who all our lives have been driven by unrealistic expectations, a tendency exacerbated by the competitive nature of occupational pursuits. When professional or business years are past, having "finished the yet unfinished," we are troubled by the unrecoverable opportunity, the unfulfilled expectations. Shouldn't there be a second chance? I can attest to this, for even now I catch myself thinking about the unfulfilled as though it were still possible (if only I devote myself more earnestly to the challenge!).

We are reminded of Sisyphus, the mythical hero condemned by Zeus to eternally push an enormous boulder up a steep slope. Time after time he neared the top, only to have the stone roll back to the bottom. Does this not describe the dreams of men who are driven by thoughts of the finish that is never finished? We were so near the top but could never quite get there and now time is gone, the opportunity lost. In theologian Roger Mehl's terse word, retirement brings "an end, but not a fulfillment."

Looking to the End

For the man who contemplates life deeply, acceptance of the unfulfilled translates as the prefiguration of death—the end-point of all earth's unfinished things.

Different from all previous transitions in adult life, retirement brings with it a sense of finality; there remains only the specter of uncertainty relative to whatever lies beyond life as we know it. For non-Christians this is like entering a tunnel with no light at the end—a fearsome prospect indeed! For Christians, while the unfulfilled is difficult to accept, the prospect of a completely fulfilled life in heaven beyond beckons brightly. Hence we can be satisfied with something less than fulfillment here.

For those to whom retirement is little more than a pleasurably passive existence made up of socializing, minor projects, and diversions of one kind or another, the approaching specter of the end is bound to create one of life's dominant fears. Little now remains that can be deemed ultimately purposeful to such a life. If present living is characterized by merely marking time with insignificant things, time will move ever more cumbersomely, albeit inexorably and swiftly.

Rather than try to cope with such a fearful prospect, some choose the way of denial or meaningless busyness. Others, for whom hope is not a sustaining strength, deteriorate rapidly in health or in mental acuity. For the person who demands optimal personal fulfillment from the here and now, the specter of the end also carries the same fear. For even the record of past successes and joys is dimmed by the looming expectation of the end of all things.

For the non-Christian, death is seen as the time when all unfulfilled hopes are dashed forever. What is unfinished shall remain forever unfinished. In stark contrast, for the Christian death is really birth into life eternal, signifying not an end but a beginning. For the Christian, the unfinished can be left behind with assurance that hopes for true personal fulfillment shall be realized in the perfection of the life above. While keeping eternity's values in view, the Christian can use the remaining time as opportunity to serve the Lord of life. Additionally, there is the attendant assurance that what God appoints and expects of us is achievable within the limits he appoints. So age and time are not factors to stand in our way. What he asks of us is accompanied by his enablement.

Do we not all have friends who say, "I never think about my death"? Even in later years, some men keep very busy, having important professional or business interests. With sufficient financial assets, reasonably good health, and a busy lifestyle, it's not difficult to dismiss thoughts of impending death. Roger Gould says, "As though there was a pact with the world: if we worked hard and succeeded and made proper sacrifices along the way, we would never be overcome by the fear that all this would be annihilated one day. Work enabled us to sanitize the fear of our own mortality."[2]

Curiously, individuals with this mind-set often have no plans to retire—ever. It's as though, by continuing whatever they're engaged in, immunity is granted from having to face the end of all things earthly, one's own life included. But can those who do not retire escape forever the ultimate questions as to the meaning of it all?

What we have here is an illusion. Continuation in work represents continuation of a working person's value. Work accomplished is seen as health to the person working. The power of one's position is seen as the power to live on.

When a man reaches retirement, one thing is certain whether he gives thought to it or not; he's entered life's final period. At some point he will cross over into eternity. The unfinished comes to its finish!

Seeing the Unfinished as Failure

We struggle against the unfulfilled and the unfinished because we tend to view them as personal failures. It is a mistake, however, to equate success only with tasks that were completed and objectives that were reached!

How are we to deal with past failures—whether real or imagined? The Christian should look at the apostle Paul as an example. When he reached the finish of his ministry he could say, "As for me, I feel that the last drops of my life are being poured out for God. The glorious fight that God gave me I have fought, the course that I was set I have finished, and I have kept the faith. The future for me holds the crown of righteousness which God, the true judge, will give to me in that day—and not, of course, only to me but to all those who have loved what they have seen of him" (2 Tim. 4:6–8 *Phillips*).

To its end, Paul's life was an investment in the kingdom of God—his life a ministry wherever he was and whatever the circumstances. In human terms, not all of it was successful. His life drew near its end in prison, where he knew death awaited him. Some of his most precious, most positive thoughts come to us from his confinement there. In his prison letter to the church at Philippi, he urges all believers to learn the life of rejoicing, even as he himself is overjoyed with his status "in Christ." No sense of the unfinished could deter the great apostle from his ultimate joy. With one foot planted on earth, the other in heaven, the meaning of his personal being was established in the life of eternity. He was unconcerned with what probably he considered unfinished ministry. Others were coming along to take it up—like young Timothy. His own times were in God's hands. There was nothing to fear. When it came time to pass on the mantle to others, it would be the right time. God is in control of all things. He makes no mistakes!

The Christian should not look on retirement as the end of living. He's not moving toward an end, save an earthly end. Thus, to use Paul's term, he is preparing for his "departure." He's looking to the kingdom of God and his eternal residence with the Lord and all the redeemed people of God, fully aware of the Scripture that says "For here we have no lasting city, but we seek the city which is to come" (Heb. 13:14). Much like victory over sin and self-centeredness, his personal growth, even his service for God, is only partially realized. But he rejoices in the prospect of being made whole in Christ in the life to come. So as long as life here continues, he wishes only to be a positive witness to his Lord's grace and goodness.

Viktor Frankl stressed the place of meaning in a person's life. He develops the theme that man everywhere seeks meaning for his life and lives to fulfill himself in accordance with that meaning.[3] The confusion that affects the retiree comes as he looks back on the unfinished aspects of his career and supposes that any significance of his life concluded there. He fails to grasp the fact that personal meaning advances without interruption. His task is to know for sure where that meaning is found.

Unfinished Relationships

Part of the unfinished that overtakes us in retirement is unfinished relationships—those severed by some event such as death or divorce or perhaps by alienation or neglect. With leisure to contemplate the loss in a clearer light, it can be seen which of these unfinished relationships requires attention. It may be the relationship with a family member that needs mending or with a friend that needs to be deepened. Recovering or repairing a relationship can be a major advance toward fulfillment.

When a dear one dies, one of life's most meaningful attachments is left incomplete, with no further possibility for completion. In the end, all human attachments are left uncompleted. To those who perceive death as the end, this is a dreadful thought. For Christians there is the blessed hope of a reunion in heaven, when the relationship, though not the same as on earth, will be a relationship truly completed.

Saying Yes to God for All Things

Accepting the unfulfilled and the unfinished and moving on to use retirement years wisely is to say "yes" to all we've received from God's hand. Let me illustrate. E. Stanley Jones, late world Christian statesman and evangelist to many lands, wrote a helpful little book with the aid of his daughter and her husband when he was in his late eighties and physically impaired. The book, last of many, was entitled *The Divine Yes*.[4]

Jones tells a story that has some parallels with my own. He recounts a conversation with a retired Methodist bishop who was restless and frustrated.

Whether the bishop fully recognized it or not, what troubled him was his being no longer in the limelight. He was no longer a recognized person, publicly prominent. Conscious of a need, his question to Dr. Jones had to do with knowing the secret of victorious living at such a time as this.

"It is," said Jones, "in self-surrender, in giving up the innermost self to Jesus." The problem, Jones pointed out, was in the texture of the things that held his bishop friend. When the outer strands were broken by retirement, the inner strands were not enough to hold him. Then Jones gave his own witness to the truth of what he was talking about. At age eighty-seven, he had had a stroke and was consigned to living with insurmountable handicaps—impairment of vision, hearing, speech, locomotion, use of one arm.

This was in 1971. He was to live for fourteen months in this condition. "The glorious thing was that my faith was not shattered. I was not holding it; it was holding me." To the bishop, Jones pointed out that when in his own life the outer strands were cut by this stroke, life didn't shake because it was held by the inner strands. His message: When we don't possess faith, faith possesses us. When we seem not to possess God, he possesses us! When life is shouting a human "no," there is a divine "yes" that resounds even louder.

Just before he died at age eighty-nine, Jones gave this final testimony: "I can't afford to be anything but grateful that He thought enough of me to give me this period at the end of life to be a proof that what I've spoken about—the unshakeable Kingdom and the unchanging Person—is true because I'm showing it to be true by His grace."[5]

Acceptance of retirement doesn't mean resignation, nor is it retreat into apathy and disinterest. It cannot be mere consent to "what life now affords"; these are all passive responses, not really saying "yes." Acceptance is active response—or to adopt Paul Ricoeur's term, "active personal surrender." In E. Stanley Jones's words, it is "giving up the innermost life to Jesus."

Now, when we connect "active" with "surrender," as Ricoeur does, are we combining opposites? I think not. We must see surrender as giving oneself over to something or someone. To do so meaningfully is to take the initiative, to actively take on whatever we're giving ourselves to. Surrender also implies redirection—not necessarily in terms of something less, only in terms of something "different." Here is acceptance and affirmation at its finest and fullest, letting God make known his perfect plan for this time of life and answering the divine "yes" with the human "yes."

In retirement we come much closer than at any other time to accepting our own mortality, to saying "yes" to our own impending death, making an active personal surrender to the inevitability of life's earthly end. During our working years, how readily most of us dismissed the notion of imminent mortality.

In searching for the meaning of death, the German philosopher Heidegger also saw it as interrupting life, making life incomplete. That would be right if we look only at this side of the grave, not beyond. The Christian sees further! His vision reaches into eternity!

Heidegger was unable to see life's incompleteness as life completed in eternity with God our Savior. We who are Christ's can accept incompleteness now because it leads to the ultimate completion! We can turn away from our unfulfilled life-long career and make an active personal surrender to Jesus, with the prospect of the fulfillment of self in the kingdom of God. For this we are making preparation now—in retirement.

As I write this chapter I have just finished reading Michael Cassidy's excellent book, *The Passing Summer*, a history and policy approach to the agony of South Africa today—black rage, white fear, and the politics of love. In his final chapter entitled "No Continuing City," he writes, "For if we do not live under the aspect of eternity we will be corrupted into thinking that earth is our home. . . ."[6] Cassidy includes two quotes relevant to our subject. The first is from C. S. Lewis, who wrote in *God in the Dock*: "If men indeed exist for the glory of God, then their final end and their destiny as persons is not to be found in this passing world."[7] The second is Malcolm Muggeridge's word, "The only ultimate disaster that can befall us is to feel ourselves at home in this world."[8]

Sometimes futility in retirement lies in trying "to feel at home in this world." Retirement might better be the time we wean ourselves away from assuming that our destiny resides in anything realized in this passing world. How truly Goethe observed that "those who do not hope for another life are always dead to this one." The Christian's hope in Christ keeps his spirit alive through every change! What may seem so uncertain takes on ultimate certainty through faith in the One who plans the whole of our lives both in time and for eternity. The strategy lies in taking each day as he gives it, and in giving him back the day-by-day control.

Just because we come to realize our true home is not in this passing world, does the world then become a less exciting place in which to live for the present? Or is there less reason to see what God is doing in our world? Have we retired from utilizing a healthy curiosity? Have we renounced appreciation for all he's blessed us with? Shouldn't our interests embrace as much of this world as possible, right up to our leaving it for the next? Retirement affords this grand opportunity.

It is the sad case that many retirees, even though they have financial means and health to travel abroad, fail to see the wonders of God's hand in the great diversity that makes up his world. There are others who are unable to travel but are enthralled with the wonders they observe all around them. It's a difference in outlook. Which type of person will you be?

The freedom we gain in retirement is freedom to exercise a maturing personal power as never before. It has nothing at all to do with power in the workplace—organizational power, social, economic, or political power—the same power that once resided in title, position, rank, or prominence. Neither is it the power of economic means, nor that which is assimilated from being in the company of influential people. It has solely to do with power to be the person God wants us to be, power to grow and to advance in our experience of human fulfillment as part of his family. It is inner power—power from God through his Spirit, power to live positively, joyfully, fruitfully. It is power to fulfill God's best in our being, our relationships, and our service. That's power as power is intended to be!

Retirement should find us advancing in an ever-deepening maturity—both spiritual and social. Included here should be breadth of mind, depth of spirit, and wider understanding of the world we inhabit with all its needs and sorrows. We should be maturing in compassion, with a growing sense of what God is doing in our time.

There's a mistaken notion abroad that retirement is the end of having definite goals to drive our lives forward, that there is no longer anything to struggle for, to aspire toward—no particular ends we must concentrate our efforts to attain, no mountains to climb. But then, what better way to lose life's vitality, to be cheated of some special purposes! Provisional and tentative though some of these latter-day goals may be, they're genuinely meant to activate us toward reaching beyond ourselves and in the process to exercise new vitality.

Are we not still the earthly companions of Jesus, still stewards of all he's placed in our hands, still servants in his kingdom? Then let's move beyond yesterday, seek his plan for the present, take up whatever free career he chooses to open to us! Let's begin to grow as never before!

> I do concentrate on this: I leave the past behind and with hands outstretched to whatever lies ahead I go straight for the goal—my reward the honor of being called by God in Christ.
>
> [Philippians 3:13–14 *Phillips*]

9

God's Wounded Healers

I would like to focus now on the problem that afflicts many men who are suddenly retired from active life. It is the depressive syndrome, which often afflicts men who have been prominent in professional ministry. I want to encourage you who have suffered in this way to know that your call to ministry has not been brought to a close, but perhaps only to a less demanding stage.

While my bout with mental anguish and its disorienting features is not identical with the experience of others similarly retired, cause and consequence are much the same. As I've recently addressed groups and conducted interviews, it has become evident that many of God's older servants have battled their way through something of the same crisis, adding case histories to document the commonality of this crisis of transition. Mental anguish in some form seems all too often to attend this abrupt change of master status and its many adjustments.

Because such accounts of depression are often misunderstood by Christian laypeople—some of whom think it incompatible with an obedient and faith-filled Christian life—ministers seem especially reluctant to talk about their experiences. Today, however, the large corps of trained Christian counselors and therapists frequently hear stories like these.

Historical Parallels

Any one of a number of famous preachers and theologians have suffered depressive states, from the reformer Martin Luther to the prince of preachers Charles Haddon Spurgeon. I've chosen to look at one such prominent figure, J. B. Phillips, best known for his translation of the New Testament in modern English.

In a biography coauthored by his wife and a close friend[1] we have an intimate personal look at a man whose years of mental anguish speak to others who have experienced the same darkness. For our encouragement, Phillips's experience doesn't leave us in a shared depression but points the way "up and out." What reassurance there is for us to know, first, that we are not alone in such afflictions, and second, that God will meet us in our blackest hours—added proof that God is there for us.

Phillips's prolific correspondence shows that even during the time Phillips was battling anxiety and depression, suffering mental torment, he was guiding others through their shadowed episodes of doubt and desperation.

Unlike my brief experience of a few days, Phillips suffered on and off through the length of his adult life. Soon after his ordination in 1930 he underwent therapeutic treatment with the eminent British psychiatrist Leonard Browne. For months at a stretch he knew relative release, only to be thrown back into mental turmoil again and again. He was indeed "a wounded healer," a fellow struggler, one with us who, although he had been used of God to help in the healing process of others, was himself deeply wounded in spirit.

At numerous points, Phillips's description matches in detail my own experience, so much so that I found myself unable to read his account until I'd begun a genuine recovery. The association of inner pain was too great. In fact, I asked Ruth to put the book out of sight so I would not be reminded of it. Later it became a welcome part of my mental and emotional reemergence. Particular therapeutic agents, it is true, can only be used at certain strategic times.

Phillips the Perfectionist

J. B. Phillips was a serious, introspective perfectionist, not unlike many highly dedicated ministers who desire to be their absolute best for God. In childhood, Phillips's father instilled in him the need to be perfect. This was to plague him ever afterward in what he regarded the inadequacy of all his work. This despite universal recognition of his writings in the whole of the English-speaking world.

Although unsure of the precise meaning of Jesus' saying, "Be ye perfect," Phillips felt these words gave support to his father's expectation of perfection in him. Inability to reach the impossible standard was, in his judgment, failure. As he applied the standard to himself, there could be no degrees of success and failure; it was not a matter of degrees. Thus, all his life he feared criticism, feared he might not be the perfect husband, the perfect minister. He feared being laughed at. As much as fearing failure itself, he feared the very perception of failure.

Whenever Phillips was compared less favorably with others, he plunged into dark jealousy. In one note he tersely penned: "Rather die than be ordinary." Three months later his correspondence carried this word: "I just can't bear anyone to criticize me, any- one to see me fail."[2] The worst disaster that could overtake him was to be thought less than perfect, yet always there was the feeling of insecurity. Such impossible expectations could of course only shatter the realization of his best hopes. Whereas his faults were common enough, the resulting degree of self- recrimination was excessive.

Three years into his ministry, Phillips barely sur- vived a serious operation. As he hovered between life and death, he had a dream, which he later described in his autobiography as a dream that filled him with such anxiety and distress that he referred to it often as "one of life's darkest moments." He speaks with great relief of a biblical text, "The Lord, he it is that doth go before thee." He credits this biblical promise with saving him from total despair at that time.

The Terrible Standard

Isn't it true that ministers especially feel that they must lead lives above criticism, that they must fully embody all they preach and teach? Their very vocation demands a higher degree of piety and self-control than is expected of other people. Often, New Testament admonitions such as those found in the Epistles of Timothy and Titus are used to justify this exceedingly high standard. Thus human failure and fault seem magnified when manifested in those who teach the holiness of God and the victorious life in Christ. Can we possibly calculate the clergy casualties that result from this mentality?

Curiously, in Phillips's personality there emerged an opposite yet correlated side—his sense of being superior to other people. Undoubtedly these claims were supported by his drive for perfection, but each time he was faced with his pride he was ashamed of the twin reality—his conceit.

Phillips was from the beginning a successful parish priest and when he sent his contemporary paraphrase of Colossians to his friend C. S. Lewis, he was encouraged by Lewis to go on translating all the Epistles. His pioneer work, *Letters to Young Churches*, brought him worldwide recognition. Macmillan, his American publisher, soon sold over a million copies of his books, sales that eventually surpassed the six million figure in world sales. But his response was only to say, "What I've actually done appears as nothing vis-à-vis the Terrific Standard."[3]

In and out of psychiatric clinics, Phillips referred often to his being reduced to helpless tears, to agonizing restrictions on his active ministry, which was often disabled by his mental distress. He refers to suffering the limiting disabilities of gastritis and diarrhea, symptoms all too familiar to those who have suffered acute anxiety and depression.

With book sales in the millions and his fame growing, doors opened wide to minister to individuals through correspondence. Indefatigably, he responded to letters from all quarters of the world. From every continent, untold numbers of people were comforted and guided by his notes of counsel and encouragement. This brought neither cheer nor release to his own spirit. He struggled on. While a few knew of that struggle, most did not, for he was unable to share it with but a few confidants. What a lesson this is—the need we all have for a confidant with whom to share our deepest afflictions of spirit!

Looking back on my own dark valley, I too was reduced at times to helpless tears, to abdominal symptoms—all a simple consequence of mental anguish. I too was often unable to find cheer even in opportunities for ministry to others. I too experienced this terrifying feeling of being confined, restricted—in my study, in the house, in the community. At one point in Phillips's despair, his doctor wrote him asking if he had any feeling of constriction around the head, any sense of being shut in and needing to get out of a confined space. It was this very same sense that all but terrified me at times, the almost violent need to get out of the house. Feeling physically and spatially hemmed in was a manifestation of the terrible confinement of spirit I was feeling within.

The sense of being confined is in part a drawing inside of oneself, shutting out the larger world. It is a creation of mental walls. What exacerbates the condition is the subconscious choice to live without windows open to a world now largely relinquished. In my case, I denied any possible thought of still being useful ("Well, thank you, but you know I'm retired now"). Because it was painful even to think about, I shut out possible avenues of service altogether, always justifying this action with the flimsiest of excuses.

Turning inward is, of course, one way of refusing risks and rewards that come as one moves into unfamiliar territory with its new requirements and opportunities. Being older and no longer in the familiar routines of professional life may mean fearing to take risks with what is less known. Actually, this is refusing the very healing that comes to us through reaching beyond ourselves to others. How often our own actions return to affect us either in health-giving or health-restricting ways!

There is a striking resemblance between another of Phillips's responses and my own. While he had difficulty enduring the days, he dreaded the nights. The second half of almost every night of his life was shot through with such mental pain, fear, and horror that he frequently had to wake himself up in order to restore some sort of balance. He commented that if he didn't manage to do that, it quite often took him three or four hours after waking to recover anything like a normal attitude towards life.

I can identify with this as well. Although my own experience was short-lived and not repeated beyond that initial week, there were fearsome night terrors, coming when all the familiar surroundings of the day were withdrawn by the darkness of night. It is then that the mind is free to roam without conscious guidance or restraints. There are no familiar sights or sounds, no surrounding movement, no limiting borders. The mind can go back in time if it chooses, create a world made up of images from the past—all unrelated and in confusing array. Or a fearful future can appear as vivid reality. There seems no limit to images the imagination can construct, and we know not whence they come. It is these unreal images that induce fear and anxiety.

As with Phillips, I found that relief comes with rising up, whatever the time of night, and seeking to engage myself with something—anything. Just break the agonizing pattern of thoughts, taking comfort and assurance in familiar surroundings that can be seen by light. Victims of such terrors know they are irrational, but it takes more than knowledge to enable them to cope.

It is often at such a time, in the dark of night, locked into strange thoughts and feelings, which in themselves are irrational and ill-defined, that there is an accompanying sense of confinement that is all but overwhelming. One feels strangely tossed about in the wildest ways. Life seems as though it were made up of purely random occurrences without meaning. Such are night visions. The urge is to flee, to get away! Yes, a depressed spirit often brings with it an unusual sense of being confined, of surrounding threats, of life being squeezed out.

I found it easy to relate to Phillips when he speaks of how severely his mental pain must have impacted his wife, Vera, who stood by him so steadfastly. The thought of imposing such a load of care on her brought feelings of guilt. I recounted this feature of my depression earlier—a feeling that would swing between gratitude for the steadfast support of my wife and guilt-laden thoughts of the unbearable weight being placed on her, knowing that her physical and emotional well-being was being put at risk too.

Another specter Phillips endured came with his recognition that while his intellectual powers seemed quite unaffected by his struggle with depression, this was not consistently true of his spiritual powers. He experienced a gradual loss of the sense of God's nearness, and was strangely unconcerned about other people. Even while ministering to others he would become more and more ingrown, hence more and more distant in spirit from those he sought to help. He knew that "perfect love casts out fear," but he was finding the reverse, that fears were diminishing his powers to love.

Is it typical for depression to affect spiritual strength? Indeed it is. I never lost my sense of God's nearness nor did I doubt his willingness and power to see me through, but for a while I was unable to reach out to others. Time and again I was able to lean on his abiding presence and find some measure of release. I could not, however, be truly concerned for others. I wasn't even aware of their needs most of the time.

Depression brings with it a radical focus on self, on one's own pains and disabilities; this becomes an overriding obsession. There is such total drawing into self that little energy is left to expend on others. As life normalized for me again, concern for others returned, but it took time. It takes time for one's thinking and emotional life to stabilize.

Principalities and Powers

Phillips recognized that at least in part he was dealing with what Scripture calls principalities and powers. I too felt strong intimations that in my vulnerability and weakness Satan was seeking entrance. I knew from Scripture that he could attack but not gain entrance. How strengthening to learn the practical truth that indeed "greater is He who is in you than he who is in the world" (1 John 4:4 NASB). At times like these, how grateful we may be that the Holy Spirit himself both protects us from satanic influences and intercedes on our behalf—that Satan is no match for God's Spirit! Even when we are too weak to pray, or when the will to pray is absent, he prays on our behalf, taking our needs to the Father in his own imploring power. He is the promised Intercessor, and he perfectly fulfills his function (see Rom. 8:26).

In response to a letter Phillips received at a time when he felt the powers of evil were arrayed against him, he advised what I have often reiterated, that one concentrate one's thoughts and prayers on our Savior Jesus Christ, assured that he will, without fail, defeat all attacks of the devil. Phillips was convinced that it serves no purpose to think about Satan's strategies, but rather one should look to Jesus—as we sing in the hymn, "Turn your eyes upon Jesus, look full in His wonderful face; and the things of earth will grow strangely dim in the light of his glory and grace."

It seems inevitable that the enemy of men's souls will seek to further undo us when we are physically and mentally weak, but Phillips's word is a sound bit of counsel, that ours is a battle of faith, and faith ultimately will triumph.

Elements of Full Recovery

I've mentioned how the fullness of recovery is signaled by a new ability to comfortably and easily share the dark experience with others. While this was true in my own case, it did not come quite so readily for Phillips. He liberally shared his experience but never was able to turn this into a means of self-help as others seem able to do.

Like Phillips, in my own recovery process I went from darkness to "a great light." When you emerge

from depression, you move literally from inner
darkness to inner light. Equally, every part of your
surroundings takes on a brighter hue. Life is "lighted
up." As depression is a time of darkness, recovery is
an experience of light—new self-affirmation, new
hope and purpose, new direction, new ability to see
the options God is setting before you.

Phillips experienced the same problem that
plagued me for so long—even after I had recovered
from the immediate crisis—the tendency to look back
in time, to seek to relive the past, to find somewhere
back there the answer to the present. Phillips once
addressed this tendency when responding to a woman
who had lost her sense of purpose after a long siege
of caring for an ill husband. He urged her to look back
with thankfulness for those times when she was useful and self-giving but cautioned her that to look back
and feel nothing but misery for no longer being able
to do what she once did is surely soul-destroying. He
suggested that our heavenly Father would be far better pleased if we took each day as it comes with
courage and good cheer. He added in closing, "So do
hold on and keep the flag flying; the King is still in
residence!"[4] Don't you love that!

Part of my own struggle has been to accept the possibility that my work is now finished, that there is
nothing of significance for me to engage in, at least
not in terms of active ministry. Phillips's correspondence indicates how difficult this problem was for
him, and I suspect this is not easy for any retiring pro-

fessional. This does not mean, however, that there is not something of true significance to occupy us.

Sharing the Dereliction of Our Lord

In a rather profound word to a correspondent, Phillips comes to an aspect of mystery in our relationship to our Savior, a mystery that clouds our thoughts when we are depressed or anxious: "I think one is sharing at those times in the dereliction of our Lord."[5] Phillips pointed to Jesus bearing the pain and terror and helplessness of all those who through the centuries have known terrible, inhuman agony and fear—the torn and broken spirits of all humanity through all ages.

In another context Phillips pointed to Jesus' agony in Gethsemane, and how he cried out, "My God, why hast Thou forsaken me?" It was a genuine question rising from Jesus' anguished spirit. To us it speaks of a mystery. What Phillips is getting at is how we might take succor in the thought that Jesus himself knew the mental anguish which, in his full humanity, caused him to cry out to the Father in face of a mystery the understanding of which was at that moment withheld even from him.

God's Wounded Healers All

Of one thing we can be sure—when overcome by mental anguish, when downcast or depressed, we can rest in his unfailing care. Underneath are the everlasting arms. When we feel we have no strength to hold on to him, we can be reassured that he holds us. (Remember E. Stanley Jones's testimony?) He will lift us up in due season! It is a badge of spiritual honor that we are among those who are "wounded healers."

Perhaps the question is a personal one at this juncture. Have you journeyed through a period of retirement disorientation, depression, and dysfunction? Have you moved on, taking advantage of spiritual strategies for reversing the painful consequences—freed to enjoy his presence and daily leading, able to look with bright hope to an ill-defined future? Then let's rejoice together that our God is the Healer of all, one with us, his "wounded healers."

One day we shall be with him, restless no longer—TRULY HOME! One day we shall no longer be the weak and easily depressed creatures of time and circumstance—TRULY WHOLE! Then as the familiar hymn says, "we shall shout and sing the victory!"

Lest we overemphasize "wounded" to the neglect of "healers," what word need we add in closing? Whether we continue blessedly active or suffer great limitations, Simone de Beauvoir has that word for us: To the active she would say, "There is only one solution if old age is not to be an absurd parody of our former life, and that is to go on pursuing ends that give our existence a meaning—devotion to individuals, to groups or to causes, social, political, intellectual or creative work. In spite of the moralists' opinion to the contrary, in old age we should wish still to have passions strong enough to prevent us turning in upon ourselves." And to the more limited she would say,

"One's life has value so long as one attributes value to the life of others, by means of love, friendship. . . . When this is so, then there are still valid reasons for activity or speech."[6] So indeed it is our touch with others that allows us to be the person God wants us to be, permits us to be, and then blesses us in being. Wounded? Perhaps, but wounded healers indeed!

> For He Himself has said, *"I will never leave you nor forsake you."* So we may boldly say: *"The Lord is my helper; I will not fear."*
>
> [Hebrews 13:5, 6 NKJV]

10

With Eternity's Values in View

I invite you to reflect with me on the most important questions a retired Christian can raise: In retrospect, looking over the length and events of my lifetime, what is the deepest longing of the human heart? Is this longing satisfied by anything life on earth can bring? How does it compel us to look beyond retirement, so that the purposes we pursue during retirement bring spiritual reassurance, hence make that stage of life fully satisfying?

I encourage you to read Peter Kreeft's *Heaven: The Heart's Deepest Longing*, which speaks to these questions.[1]

We've been tracing at some depth the last stage of life when, having laid down his lifework, a man is faced with such fundamental questions as, Who am I? How shall my final years be lived meaningfully in terms of God's claim on my life? As my years shorten, and losses begin to surpass gains, how shall I live with eternity's values in view?

What better time than the less-harried years of retirement for a man to think through the whole of life's meaning, making the approaching end a part of his overall evaluation of life's important issues? It is then that he can reflect on the deepest longing of his life. Is it a longing left unrecognized in the scramble to find substitute satisfactions? Is this longing something briefly and superficially pondered off and on but never in depth? Is this unnamed longing one that someday will indeed be fulfilled? If so, when? How?

Malcolm Muggeridge claimed, paradoxically, to find his chief blessing in his deepest sorrow. He speaks of our alienation, of our being strangers in a strange land—displaced persons in this world. This he calls "the greatest of all blessings" and explains, "The only ultimate disaster that can befall us, I have come to realize, is to feel ourselves to be at home here on earth. As long as we are aliens, we cannot forget our true homeland."[2]

Earthly dissatisfaction and restlessness may prove the road by which we arrive at what shall prove our truest satisfaction, the realization of our highest hopes, the object of our settled faith, the attainment of our true homeland. This notion is supported by the famous declaration of St. Augustine in his *Confessions:* "Thou hast made us for thyself and our hearts are restless until they rest in thee." Centuries of Christian thought affirm this truth that the way to true rest is restlessness. Rest for our spirits is not only found in

God, but in recognizing he has prepared a place for us—heaven. For heaven is our ultimate and abiding home. How often our retirement home is something less than what we've enjoyed in previous years. We settle for some latter-day compromise. Smaller quarters may seem more appropriate to our retirement needs yet may produce unexpected dissatisfaction—easier to manage and to get around, yes, but not enough room for things we wish to keep. C. S. Lewis says, "Your place in heaven will seem to be made for you and you alone, because you were made for it."[3] Jesus said, "I go to prepare a place for you." How wonderful! But this is not a place we now can see.

Throughout this book I've traced the matter of personal identity, noting how it is formed and how later on it is often lost in the retirement transition. Our true identity, however, was lost in Eden. Sin separated us from God in whose image we had been created, and for whose glory we were to live our lives. In Eden our alienation from God occurred, as well as alienation from brother man and alienation from ourselves. Henceforth, throughout man's long history, he was destined to struggle with this all-embracing alienation. It is this alienation from God that brought about our true identity problem Yet our lost Eden was not our true and abiding home. It is heaven, our true home, that will restore that pristine identity. Unless heaven is part of the retirement perspective, retirement loses its most precious end. And when this is so, time becomes an enemy and aging becomes a fearful prospect, however healthy we are, however youthful we feel. The final years are meant to be more precious, not less. As Christians, we are to feel more released, not more closed in, as time moves on. We are to feel more confident, less threatened, because we look forward to heaven as our home. The crux of it all is expressed in Kreeft's question: "Time is our country of exile; how do we get home to eternity?"[4] Without the assurance of an eternal home, our time on earth is indeed little more than occupying a country of exile, with all the forebodings that exile represents to the human spirit. Is this not the issue that presses on the mind and soul of every thoughtful Christian retiree?

How true it is that we have a nostalgia for that which was lost in Eden, centering as it did in the bliss of the intimate presence of God. We are to be like Moses of whom we read, "he endured as seeing him who is invisible" (Heb. 11:27). The same writer, in "the faith chapter," tells of the Israelites acknowledging that they were but strangers and exiles on the earth. Then he adds, "But as it is, they desire a better country, that is, a heavenly one" (Heb. 11:16). Then he applies it to us, "For here we have no lasting city, but we seek the city which is to come" (Heb. 13:14). The older we grow the more we recognize we have no lasting city, no lasting situations to take refuge in. We are pilgrims on a swiftly passing sojourn.

Earth Haunted by Heaven

Kreeft introduces the intriguing notion of earth being haunted by heaven.[5] This "haunting" leads us to expect to see the invisible, to know the unknowable—the very real presence of God. It is the realm of the eternal, spiritual world to come that enables us to see all our life-stages and transitions in proper perspective.

Why do many people go through an endless succession of earthly attachments and commitments to causes and to things such as material possessions, sexual fulfillment, and personal recognition, even after repeated experience tells them they are and will always be disappointed? Kreeft reminds us that we keep trying despite repeated failures because we're looking for God, but we're looking in the wrong places.

Pascal put it somewhat differently in his observation that "the infinite abyss [our passionate desire for the things of earth] can be filled only with an infinite and immutable object, in other words with God himself."[6] He spoke, you recall, of that God-formed vacuum in the soul of man. The race has proved in every age the truth of this observation.

Is it any wonder that throughout life we search for things that are immutable, things that will not turn out to be transient in their ability to satisfy? Yet, always we search in vain. All earthly joys—none excepted—are transient. No earthly place or situation can satisfy man's deepest longing. Nothing of earth can truly satisfy the longing heart, only God himself.

How, then, shall we know him, the living God? Through a personal faith-relationship with the Lord Jesus Christ, we know God personally as the eternal Father. By faith, we are at one with him. As nothing less than God himself can satisfy the human soul, and since the Lord Jesus is himself the revelation of the Father, he is rightfully the object of every longing heart.

In Scripture we who trust the Savior are said to be "heirs of God and fellow heirs with Christ" (Rom. 8:17). If heirs, then, of course, we have an inheritance. Peter speaks of this: "an inheritance which is imperishable, undefiled, and unfading, kept in heaven for you, who by God's power are guarded through faith for a salvation ready to be revealed in the last time" (1 Peter 1:4–5). Hebrews 9:15 calls it "the promised eternal inheritance."

We know something of heaven for we know the Lord of heaven and have placed our faith in him as our Savior. He said he was going to prepare a place for us, and that he would come and take us to himself that where he is we shall be also (see John 14:3). Yes, heaven is home! Our home! Our true and only home! Already, we are told, eternal life abides in us (see John 3:36).

C. S. Lewis: An Exquisite Argument

There is the well-known argument of C. S. Lewis. His major premise is that every innate desire in us has a corresponding object that satisfies that desire. His minor premise is that there exists in us a desire, which nothing in time, nothing on earth, can satisfy. Thus it can be concluded that there must then exist outside of time and earth that which correspondingly satisfies this deepest of desires. Is this not, presumably, God himself the Person, and heaven itself the place?

This truth of God the Person, heaven the place is brought together in Jesus' promise to the disciples in John 14:3, where he says, "And when I go and prepare a place for you, I will come again and will take you to myself, that where I am you may be also." Note "a place . . . where I am." The person and the place are for the Christian the object of the heart's deepest longing.

Lewis places this overarching desire over against all other desires as "an unsatisfied desire which is itself more desirable than any other satisfaction." Moreover, the reality of the object is implicit in the desire. And the crux of the argument is this: "If I find in myself a desire which no experience in this world can satisfy, the most probable explanation is that I was made for another world."[7]

Lewis has provided the argument that speaks to the restlessness we all know, the restlessness that becomes acute and painful to the Christian retiree who has laid down his career, taken on a free existence with unbearable amounts of leisure time to fill (not kill), and desperately wants to know what life will mean in its whole course right on to its appointed earthly end. No greater question confronts him than "How can I live before God so as to prepare myself to see God's face in the near future? How can I live with eternity's values in view?"

As in all things human, there is a dark side that must not be overlooked. It might be called the "residual inner contradiction." The apostle Paul speaks of it in Galatians chapter five, and especially verse seventeen. He points to the flesh/spirit dichotomy that characterizes every genuine believer until the time of his departing his earthly life. The apostle says, "For the desires of the flesh are against the Spirit, and the desires of the Spirit are against the flesh; for these are opposed to each other, to prevent you from doing what you would."

There is a battle raging between the flesh and the Spirit that impedes our resting in the hope of our eternal inheritance. This struggle is reflective of the inner conflict Paul describes in Romans chapter seven: what he "would do" but doesn't, what he "doesn't want to do" but does. The flesh and the Spirit struggle against contradiction.

How does this pull in two directions affect our longing for heaven? That longing is balanced against a residual human fear of things unknown and a desire to remain with what is familiar regardless of how uncertain it may be—the proclivity to cling to that which is known—the striving against the unfamiliar. As a pastor friend said to me in a conversation about our inevitable departure to be with the Lord, "It is a marvelous hope but an awesome prospect." Indeed it is! While we do not fear death, we have a natural dread of the awesome that is not easily removed, even by faith and the hope that is ours in Christ.

Our sense of personal identity is tied to things earthly—to our known earthly history. We see ourselves in the context of our earthly experience. As yet we cannot identify ourselves within the history of eternity or picture ourselves in the environs of heaven. Just as the future is not mapped out for the retiree, so heaven is not open to our eyes. We must receive it by faith, though our human tendency is to walk by sight. This is our struggle, a struggle likely to be enhanced as we approach the end of our days. But we are not left without the direction of God's Word and the enablement of God's Spirit.

It is not just that we continue to look to things earthly for our deepest satisfactions or our true identity, but the residual pull of the world is great, evermore set against the pull of the Spirit. Our victory, once more, comes as we continue in God's Word, in the striving of prayer, in ever-renewed surrender to the Spirit's control of mind and spirit.

The apostle further enables us in our understanding through his word to the Corinthians, "What no eye has seen, nor ear heard, nor the heart of man conceived, . . . God has revealed to us through the Spirit" (1 Cor. 2:9–10). This is followed by a word of assurance that we who are in Christ do have the Spirit and his ministry that enables us to understand spiritual truth.

As Christian retirees it is our task and privilege to devote time to eternal realities. Whatever engages us, let it be with eternity's values in view. Let neither fear nor doubt keep us from the promise of the life awaiting us.

The apostle Paul instructed the Christians at Colossae to live their lives by the power of the risen Christ, words never more aptly applied than to Christian retirees:

> If you are then "risen" with Christ, reach out for the highest gifts of Heaven, where your master reigns in power. Give your heart to the heavenly things, not to the passing things of earth. For, as far as this world is concerned, you are already dead, and your true life is a hidden one in Christ. One day, Christ, the secret center of our lives, will show himself openly, and you will all share in that magnificent dénouement.
>
> [Colossians 3:1–4 *Phillips*]

11

Give Me This Mountain!

G od's ultimate desire, it seems clear, is to have us move on in our retirement years to becoming overcomers—above all, spiritual overcomers and in consequence, overcomers through every daily demand. Indeed, while for some these may prove difficult years, severely limiting years, they need not be self-defeating years. If in the eternal habitations the best is yet to be, the approaching night is only the harbinger of that day "which breaks eternal bright and fair." Whatever losses we sustain as we grow older, promised gains will infinitely outnumber those losses. Recall the great apostle saying to the Philippians, "I count everything as loss because of the surpassing worth of knowing Christ Jesus my Lord" (Phil. 3:8). We need not believe that these last years will be marked by nothing but loss.

Because of the greater leisure we command in retirement, time can be spent learning to know Jesus better and preparing to know him fully in the life soon to be ours. Thus, however restricted life becomes, or how few the opportunities to serve him overtly, we can become true overcomers, ever growing more like him in conformity of our spirit with his. "I can do all things in him who strengthens me" (Phil. 4:13).

A Man of God to Remember

The Bible records the story of a great overcomer with whom we can relate since his greatest days were in his old age. That very special man is the Old Testament figure Caleb (see Josh. 14 and 15). God said of Caleb, "He followed me fully." Moses gave identical testimony, saying that both Joshua and Caleb "followed him fully." Caleb himself affirmed it to be true: "I wholly followed the Lord my God." The secret is out! Caleb fully followed the Lord!

The best illustration of an overcoming life is the visible witness of such a life. What more powerful incentive than when we see such a life lived out in trying times, lived out on a practical plane for all to view! How true the promise appears when we see it fleshed out in an individual's daily life!

Caleb was not an Abraham, nor a Moses, a David, or a Paul. He was just a man among men, ordinary in many respects yet living an extraordinary life, not because of favored circumstances—far from it—not because of anything superior in himself—there's no record of that. His life was extraordinary solely because of his relationship to God in whom he placed his utmost confidence—a relationship of unswerving faith and obedience.

Caleb doesn't enter the picture in Scripture until he is forty years old. In all the early chapters of the Book of Joshua, throughout the initial plans for conquest of the land, Caleb doesn't appear at all; he isn't even mentioned in the background of the narrative. Evidently, Caleb had some unusual capabilities and was absolutely trustworthy, for we learn that he was a ruler in the tribe of Judah, the largest and most important of the tribes of Israel, the one from which our Lord came in the flesh. He had endured and was in every sense a wise and mature leader, and at eighty-five wasn't through yet.

Caleb Chooses the Way of Faith

God had chosen a people for himself and had promised them a special land, Canaan, for their everlasting possession. During Caleb's time, the land had not yet become Israel's, but they were at the very gates. God invited them to possess it as his gift yet instructed them that they must take it by force, promising that he would lead and enable them in the conquest (see Num. 13–14). The people responded by asking Moses to appoint spies to appraise "the possibilities"—a blatant act of unbelief! As though God's word needed confirmation!

Think of the implications of their unbelief. Suppose their report indicated this was not the time to occupy the land? Was God really in control? Was God giving them poor directions? Perhaps he needed their input? Could they proceed on his word alone, or should they heed the spies' report?

God had already told the people that the nations occupying the land were mightier than they, but he had promised to go before them and drive their enemies from the land. They were to be of good courage. But God's word seemed less than enough for a final decision; they had to go see for themselves. Faith faltered. They would rather be judicious than obedient.

Caleb represented the tribe of Judah as one of the twelve chosen to spy out the land. The spies' report was not unanimous. There was a majority report of ten, a minority report of two. The ten pointed to insurmountable difficulties, saying, "we are not able to go up against the people." But the two who brought the minority report—Joshua and Caleb— while not minimizing the difficulties, magnified the power of the Lord to overcome those difficulties. For these two men the victory was assured, so their verdict was unhesitating. Caleb, acting as the spokesman, said, "Let us go up at once, and occupy it; for we are well able to overcome it." He would not be swayed by the fears of the ten. He was as daring as his conviction was firm. The assurance of faith impelled the verdict of obedience.

Fear will always drive out faith unless faith first moves to dispel fear; the two are incompatible. Caleb chose the faith-way and so was free of tyrannizing, paralyzing, self-defeating fear.

This spiritual overcomer said, "If the Lord delights in us, he will bring us into this land." Caleb saw everything in relationship to God, not in relationship to circumstances. His chief concern was that he so live that the Lord would be able to delight in him. Thus Caleb started with a firm conviction; this gave him confidence, and confidence brought him to firm commitment. In turn, commitment led to strong courage in the face of overwhelming odds. And underneath it all was his unshakeable consecration to the Lord. Conviction, confidence, commitment, courage, consecration!

Faithless Looking Back

Along with the ten spies, the people themselves had no heart for going in. Instead they looked back, thinking of what they had had in Egypt (albeit that was not as good as they now pretended). In Canaan all they could see were giants, not God. Implicit trust is not possible in the face of such resignation to panic and unbelief. The outward look impaired the upward look!

Curiously, not once is God mentioned in the majority report, never a word concerning his promises, nor of his miraculous power over Egypt at the Red Sea. God simply did not occupy their vision. And so they rebelled. They did not and could not enter Canaan because they would not. The spies had turned the hearts of the people. What an influence their unbelief had on so many!

The result was that all ten spies died by the plague; only two were allowed to live—Joshua and Caleb. In furthering his chosen course, God divided the people into two groups—those over and those under twenty years of age. The older group had murmured against him in unbelief. The younger ones had not been part of that evil choice. All who were over twenty, an entire generation, died in the wilderness. For forty days they had wandered aimlessly in unbelief, not wanting to enter Canaan. Then for forty years, a year for a day, those who remained alive would meditate on this faithlessness, watching their generation die one by one over that long period of time.

Caleb lived through the forty years of frustration and futility in the wilderness wanderings. He saw the older generation—his generation—die off one by one until none were alive but Joshua and himself. How sorely tempted he must have been through it all! What a useless waste of time, he may have thought, for one who had given himself to wholly follow the Lord! In what possible way was it significant to follow God in this wilderness? Should he not just resign himself to the fact that these ongoing years could only mean one thing—his own death? Or he might have quietly backed away and said, "I'm retired now, there's nothing left for me to do." But no, there's no hint that he was so tempted!

In the Wilderness but not of It

Of Joshua and Caleb we read "they lived still." They were in the wilderness but not of it; they were among the unbelievers but not of them. Eventually they were to see the land, their hearts' desire realized. Joshua's and Caleb's best years of middle life were sacrificed to the sinful rebellion of their fellow Israelites. Still, as old men, these two were to lead the entry into the land. For forty years Caleb had rested full-length on the promises and faithfulness of God. Faith anticipated the promised land. Caleb already lived in that land through faith's anticipation. As the author of Hebrews was to express it long afterward, "Faith is the assurance of things hoped for, the conviction of things not seen" (Heb. 11:1).

When the forty years of wandering had ended, Caleb was an old man of eighty-five years. Confidently, he said, "I am still as strong to this day as I was in the day that Moses sent me; my strength now is as my strength was then." The story might well have ended there with the triumphant word, "So Hebron became the inheritance of Caleb . . . because he wholly followed the Lord, the God of Israel." But there is more to learn from Caleb.

For Caleb the ongoing years were not calculated as a descent, a downward journey until death brought release. Caleb wasn't living for the day he would die. He was looking for God's very best, the crowning achievement of a life of faith and obedience right up until death came as reward to the victor, not release to the victim.

We should be like Caleb who never stopped learning about God and trusting him. God has things for us to do in our last years. There are mountains to climb by his strength. In many ways, it may be that the last years are to be our very best—despite the limitations of creeping age. Caleb believed this wholeheartedly and gave himself to the proof. What about us? Shall we expect less?

With Caleb there was no diminution of expectation although unquestionably there was diminution of outward strength. He expected life to have a glorious consummation however it came. There was to be no stagnation, no resignation, no giving up! Looking back only gave him new reason to look forward with fresh encouragement. The past was the past; the future held hope.

A Supreme Achievement at Eighty-five

So Caleb's last years were to be his very best, his supreme achievement coming—can you imagine it?—at age eighty-five. It was to be on his gray head that God would place the crown of the overcomer.

The amazing feature of it all is that the old man, with the people facing the dreaded giants, the Anakim, said "Now therefore give me this mountain." He wanted to be the one to face the Anakim! He added, "If so be the Lord will be with me, then I shall be able to drive them out" (Josh. 14:12 KJV). And he did!

Incidentally, Caleb was the only leader of the forces who fully dispossessed the enemy that day. The faith that sustained the early years became the victorious faith of the later years. Is this not how God wants it to be for each one of us?

Caleb's eyes were not on himself (he would have fainted had that been his focus). Nor were Caleb's eyes on circumstances (he then would have resigned to total defeat). Rather, his eyes were fixed on God, and his gaze held steady. He could see only triumph ahead—not the triumph of self but the triumph of a mighty God who had promised and who was as good as his promise. Faith at any age takes risk, but what is there to lose when one risks for God?

With God, Caleb was joined to the true majority. He could simply claim what God had offered, knowing full well that it was God who would effect the manner of his receiving that claim. God fulfilled his promise perfectly and on time because Caleb had fulfilled the conditions consistently and completely.

If we present-day retirees are restless, well and good, if that restlessness is our waiting for God's next move and our ready response—be it our homegoing, or a new mountain to climb. Ours is the privilege of asking him, "Show me a mountain you want me to overcome"; then asking in confident faith, "Give me this mountain." Oh, indeed, it may not be the great mountain that forever memorialized Caleb in the annals of sacred history, but it is our mountain, nevertheless, the one he wants for us. Your mountain is not my mountain, nor is mine yours, but for each of us there is a mountain to claim in his strength to crown our days.

Faith Displaces Fear

You say, "I'm afraid I'm no longer up to any mountain!" But wait! The mountain of his choosing is just right for you. Will you turn away from the mountain God sets before you, rebellious because it represents difficulty or unpleasantness? Or will you claim it as yours to overcome? Even if it is a task once thought too menial for your abilities but now fitted to your limited capacity? Will you not say yes?

As Caleb lifted his eyes heavenward, so the great apostle invites us to do the same, even as he wrote the Colossian church: "Seek the things that are above, where Christ is, seated at the right hand of God. Set your minds on things that are above, not on things that are on earth" (Col. 3:1–2).

Does this mean that we are to live out our remaining days doing nothing but gazing upward in a purely passive state? No, rather, we are to keep our gaze on him who is our strength and life, receiving from him all that we need so that we may undertake what he has for us yet to do—or be.

If we continue restless with this plan, then it is the restlessness of an unyielded spirit. This restlessness God cannot heal until we yield ourselves to him.

It is difficult for an older person to lay down the stimulating demands of work, and, yes, painful just to see the work we loved and called our own now accomplished by younger men. But life need not become narrower when the demands are less, when we are no longer among the major players. It may indeed become wider because of the new horizons we are free to see.

So Let Go and Move On!

Our great need at retirement time is to let go and move on; there's much yet to experience. We need to see the past essentially as the continuum of people and events that have made us who we are—the good that represents our past. All that remains blessed to memory is still ours to savor. What is of less worth may well be forgotten as worthless baggage. Lessons from the past are given us for application all the days of our lives. It isn't renewed excitement and over-burdening challenge that we need or really desire. It is to grow more like him and to well represent him to those who take note that we have been with him. It is our influence as mature Christians that is important now, and this right of influence is one we must earn and be continually worthy of.

Caleb's example urges us not to settle for a useless life, nor to do less than he when it is said "he wholly followed the Lord." Wherever God should lead, what-ever he calls us to do, it is both our privilege and our duty to wholly follow him. And in so doing, we can rest in the fact that he knows where to lead.

When we retire from our lifetime occupation, it isn't our identity that we lose; it is only those features of our past identity that we relinquish in order that they may be replaced by new qualities that have eternal value.

We're learning how to manage loss in the light of the greater gains that stretch ahead. There is no room for sadness here, only for the joy of the Lord. So we press on, letting every new day bring its own new mountains, its own rewards. It is this, our new iden-tity, that is going to count the most for eternity. So, my companions in retirement, why not just let go and move on!

Afterword

And now, just a word to tell you where I am at the present time. Once again, I turn to an important book.

Hannah Whitall Smith first published her classic *The Christian's Secret of a Happy Life* in 1875. Literally millions have been taught and blessed in the more than a century following publication. I was one of them when I read this book just months after my conversion at age fourteen. Toward the close of her life, she wrote her spiritual autobiography. The final chapter begins, "And now that I am seventy years old . . ." But before I quote her, let me add this personal note.

The reason I quote her words is because they reflect my own story—my life as it is in the present. I am seventy-four. During the months I've been writing this book, I've spent much of the time recovering from six surgeries to replace a failing artery in one leg. I face the same eventuality for the second leg. Breakdown of the vascular system began some fifteen years ago with retinal hemorrhages that threatened loss of vision. Today, although vision has been stabilized, the

vascular problem continues. We are constantly reminded that we inhabit a body slowly but surely losing the battle.

And so retirement remains uncertain insofar as
active service roles are concerned. I have learned
through my own crisis and the uncertainty of health
and life to rest in God's appointment. As I stated earlier in the book, the question is not what I do with
whatever time he allots so much as what I am (or to
put it more precisely—what I am becoming) in the
love and grace of my God and Savior. It is the maturing life in Christ that matters most. And so let me now
quote from Hannah Whitall Smith.

> To be seventy gives one permission to stand aloof
> from the stress of life, and to lay down all burden of
> responsibility for carrying on the work of the world;
> and I rejoice in my immunity. . . . I am more than
> happy to know that the responsibilities of the present
> generation do not rest upon me, but upon the shoul-
> ders of the younger and stronger spirits, who are
> called in the providence of God to bear them. I laugh
> to myself with pleasure at the thought, and quite
> enjoy the infirmities of age as they come upon me,
> and find it delightful to be laid aside from one thing
> after another, and to be at liberty to look on in a peace-
> ful leisure at the younger wrestlers in the world's
> arena. I cannot say that their wrestling is always done
> in the way that seems best to my old eyes, but I admire
> the Divine order that evidently lays upon each gen-
> eration its own work, to be done in its own way; and
> I am convinced that, whether it may seem to us for
> good or for ill, the generation that is passing must

give place to the one that is coming, and must keep hands off from interfering. Advice we who are old may give, and the fruits of our experience, but we must be perfectly content to have our advice rejected by the younger generation, and our experience ignored.[1]

What an antidote this is to the temptation to feel guilt when one is laid aside by health, age, or lack of opportunity! How easy it is to feel that we must be in the thick of the battle until the end! Then we miss God's design for the seasons of life, the restful contemplation of God and all his works made possible in our closing years. Retirement, whatever active role it affords—or does not afford—is the time to contemplate the concluding features of earth's concerns and the glories of the life ahead. The preparation for "going home" ought to determine all that occupies us.

Donald Barnhouse Jr. offers an excellent word: "History and time are nothing more than the framework within which God is trying to win back our trust. When limits go, they will go. Life is a big word, but life now is only a shadow of what it is intended to be. Death is the last enemy, and it will be destroyed. In the meanwhile, until that is accomplished, death will be made to serve throughout history as the gate by which we pass from this damaged life into a new and perfect life. For those who trust God, this gate has the marvelous property as you get closer to it of looking less like an exit and more and more like an entrance."[2] Don't you love that last sentence?

Here is that distinctly Christian word—*hope*. Of the three greatest things Paul mentions in 1 Corinthians 13, along with such mighty attributes as faith and love comes hope. The Christian life is built on hope. Faith engenders hope—hope for the present and the future—that nothing circumstantial can daunt. Faith and hope grasp life as it is and can see ahead beyond the unknown. Faith and hope lead to soul-rest.

Roy Fairchild, in his book *Finding Hope Again*, reminds us that hope is not mere optimism, nor is it positive thinking. Positive thinking does not engender hope; rather, hope engenders positive thinking. As Fairchild realistically observes, the person of hope is fully aware of life's losses, life's harshness, life's disappointments. He knows that hope is generated out of a tragic sense of life and is the sense of possibility. Genuine hope enlarges the significance of the present, for it is alive with possibilities.[3] Hope enables us to leave the past and grasp the unknown with full assurance that God is in it all—and for good!

With what word shall we conclude? J. Sidlow Baxter, beloved Bible teacher, in his book *Does God Still Guide?*,[4] writes these lines:

> Lord, help me clearly understand,
> My way is all by Thee foreplanned;
> And I, full-yielding to Thy will,
> Life's richest purpose may fulfil.
>
> With each new winding of the way,
> New guidance may be mine each day;

A yielded heart in daily prayer
Discerns Thy watch-care everywhere.

Each day, as I with Thee commune,
Lord, set my heart and mind attune,
To hear the inward Voice divine,
With scarce a need for outward sign.

So, guided through my earthly days,
Safeguarded thus from error's maze,
My heav'nward pilgrimage shall be
A deepening fellowship with Thee.

Notes

Introduction

1. Alex Comfort, *A Good Age* (New York: Crown Publishers, Inc., 1976), 182.

2. Jules Z. Willing, *The Reality of Retirement* (New York: William Morrow and Co., Inc., 1981).

Chapter One

1. William Bridges, *Transitions: Making Sense of Life's Changes* (Menlo Park, Calif.: Addison-Wesley Publishing Co., 1980).

2. Willing, *The Reality of Retirement*, 30.

3. John Oxenham, *Selected Poems of John Oxenham* (London: Adelphi Terrace/T. Fisher Unwin, Ltd., 1924), 52.

Chapter Two

1. Jack Hayford, *Taking Hold of Tomorrow* (Ventura, Calif.: Regal Books, 1989), 98.

Chapter Four

1. Judith Viorst, *Necessary Losses* (New York: Simon and Schuster, 1986), 290.

2. Viorst, *Necessary Losses*, 237.

3. Viorst, *Necessary Losses*, 325–26.

4. John W. James and Frank Cherry, *The Grief Recovery Handbook* (New York: Harper and Row, 1988), 4.

5. James and Cherry, *The Grief Recovery Handbook*, 13.

6. Viorst, *Necessary Losses*, 249.

7. Viorst, *Necessary Losses*, 264.

8. John Bowlby, *Attachment and Loss*, vol. 3 (New York: Basic Books, Inc., 1980), 174.

9. Archibald D. Hart, *Feeling Free* (Old Tappan, N. J.: Fleming H. Revell Co., 1979), 101ff.

Chapter Five

1. R. Butler, "The Life-Review: An Interpretation of Reminiscence in the Aged," *Psychiatry* 26 (1963): 65–76; C. N. Lewis, "Reminiscence and Self-Concept in Old Age," *Journal of Gerontology* 26, no. 2 (1971): 240-43; Marcel Proust, *The Past Recaptured* (New York: Albert and Charles Boni, 1932).

2. Willing, *The Reality of Retirement*, 30.

3. Timothy K. Jones, "Reading Life Backwards," *Christianity Today* (Sept. 22, 1989): 28–31.

4. Simone de Beauvoir, *The Coming of Age* (New York: G. P. Putnam's Sons, 1972), 405.

5. Hayford, *Taking Hold of Tomorrow*, 150.

6. Oxenham, *Selected Poems of John Oxenham*, 52.

Chapter Six

1. Lee Butcher, *Retirement without Fear* (Princeton, N. J.: Dow Jones Books, 1978).

2. Paul Tournier, *Learn to Grow Old* (New York: Harper and Row, 1971), 28.

3. Sigmund Freud, *The Major Works of Sigmund Freud* (Chicago: Encyclopedia Brittanica, Inc., 1952), 74.

4. Roger L. Gould, *Transformations: Growth and Change in Adult Life* (New York: Simon and Schuster, 1978), 318.

Chapter Seven

1. Tournier, *Learn to Grow Old*, 142.

2. Tournier, *Learn to Grow Old*, 143.

3. Nikos Kazantzakis, *Zorba the Greek* (New York: Simon and Schuster, 1952), 120–21.

Chapter Eight

1. Tournier, *Learn to Grow Old*, 169.

2. Gould, *Transformations: Growth and Change in Adult Life*, 231.

3. Viktor E. Frankl, *Man's Search for Meaning* (New York: Washington Square Press, 1963).

4. E. Stanley Jones, *The Divine Yes* (Nashville: Abingdon Press, 1975).

5. Jones, *The Divine Yes*, 85.

6. Michael Cassidy, *The Passing Summer* (Venture, Calif.: Regal Books, 1989).

7. Cassidy, *The Passing Summer*, 147.

8. Cassidy, *The Passing Summer*, 472.

Chapter Nine

1. Vera Phillips and Edwin Robertson, *J. B. Phillips: The Wounded Healer* (Grand Rapids, Mich.: William B. Eerdmans Publishing Co., 1984).

2. Phillips and Robertson, *J. B. Phillips*, 10.

3. Phillips and Robertson, *J. B. Phillips*, 17.

4. Phillips and Robertson, *J. B. Phillips*, 86.

5. Phillips and Robertson, *J. B. Phillips*, 79.

6. de Beauvoir, *The Coming of Age* (New York: G. P. Putnam's Sons, 1972), 540–41.

Chapter Ten

1. Peter Kreeft, *Heaven: The Heart's Deepest Longing* (San Francisco, Calif.: Ignatius Press, 1989).

2. Malcolm Muggeridge, *Jesus Rediscovered* (New York: Doubleday, 1979), 47–48.

3. C. S. Lewis, *The Problem of Pain* (New York: Macmillan Publishing Co., 1962), 147–48.

4. Kreeft, *Heaven: The Heart's Deepest Longing*, 75.

5. See chapter 3 of Kreeft, *Heaven: The Heart's Deepest Longing*.

6. Blaise Pascal, *Pensées* (New York: Penguin Books, 1960), 74–75.

7. C. S. Lewis, *Mere Christianity* (New York: Macmillan, 1960), 120.

Afterword

1. Hannah Whitall Smith, *The Unselfishness of God* (Princeton, N. J.: Littlebrook Publishing, Inc., 1987), 229–30.

2. Donald Barnhouse Jr., *Is Anybody up There: Flying Saucers and God* (New York: Seabury Press, 1977), 122.

3. Roy W. Fairchild, *Finding Hope Again: A Pastor's Guide to Counseling Depressed Persons* (San Francisco: Harper and Row, 1980).

4. J. Sidlow Baxter, *Does God Still Guide?* (Grand Rapids, Mich.: Zondervan Publishing House, 1971), 84.